BREAKING TAPE

BREAKING TAPE

7 Steps to Winning at Work and Life

Dennis Mankin • Karen McGraw, Ed.D.

McMan Publishing
www.mcmanpublishing.com

Cover design and graphics by Jeff Duckworth, http://www.duckofalltrades.com/
Creative support by Matt Shanor, Blue Circle Creative
Editorial support by Patricia Galagan

Published by McMan Publishing
26 Horseshoe Trail, Barnardsville, NC 28709

Library of Congress Cataloging-in-Publication Data
Mankin, Dennis
    Breaking Tape: 7 steps to winning at work and life / Dennis Mankin, Karen McGraw.
-- 1st Ed.

ISBN 978-0-9913567-0-6 (paperback); ISBN 978-0-9913567-1-3 (ebook)
I. Self-help. 2 Goals. 3. Success.

First Edition

Printed in the United States of America.

Dedications

First, I would like to thank my wife, Gwen, for her patience when I took time away from family to write, and for her creative input along the way. Secondly, I would like to express my sincere thanks to some close friends and family for their suggestions and input, including Jenna, Joan, Matthew, Becky, Christopher and my mother, as well as others. Lastly, I would like to offer my special thanks to my dear friend, colleague and co-author Dr. Karen McGraw, for having the patience and perseverance to work through this book project with me and for being the perfect balance in the equation.

Dennis Mankin
Barnardsville, NC

Ideas and innovations are all around us. But it takes special conditions to bring them forward. I dedicate this book to those in my life who encouraged me to take an idea and make it a reality. To my husband, Bruce, who tolerates my long hours and gives me the freedom to pursue my Wish; to my children—Chris, Colby, Patrick, and Marissa—who loved me in spite of the fact that I was a 'different' mom; to my own mother, a steel magnolia who helped me see I could attain my Wish; and to the many furry friends who kept me company during the work and writing process. Finally, my sincere appreciation to my friend, colleague, and co-author, Dennis Mankin, who kept us both motivated and made the job of writing together easier than I could have imagined. Thank you!

Karen L. McGraw
Austin, TX

Contents

PART ONE

Introduction & Overview

Introduction & Principles

"Never be afraid to try something new. Remember that a lone amateur built the Ark. A large group of professionals built the Titanic." – Dave Barry, author and columnist

Success—we all want it, we all seek it. You're reading this book because you desire to be more successful personally and/or professionally:

- **At work**—you want to take that next logical career step, but so far it hasn't happened
- **At home**—you want to find more personal satisfaction with the life you are living and with the people you call "family"
- **Your health and well-being**—you need to shed a few pounds (but then, you say that every year) or find better ways to deal with stress
- **Your financial situation**—you want to gain better control over your finances (so they won't control you)
- **Your relationships**—you want to be a better friend, have a better friend, and/or experience a deeper, more meaningful spiritual relationship.

Like us, you probably have set more than your fair share of goals that you either struggled to attain or abandoned. We can all relate to that. It's time for a new approach—something that will help you define the success you want. Something that will help you create a practical, easy-to-work plan to achieve success. Something that really does work! We have a plan to make this a reality for you! **Breaking Tape** gives you a proven seven-step process to help you identify, plan for, and achieve the success you envision. We call it the WINNING Method.

Purpose and Content of This Book

The purpose of this book is to teach you how to use our WINNING Method *to achieve personal or work life success.* We developed the WINNING Method to help people just like you "break the tape" at the finish line that defines their success. You will use our WINNING Method to define the success you want, and the outcomes, goals, and strategies required to achieve it. This becomes your personal plan—a step-by-step guide you will use to *break the tape* on your work and life success.

The chapters in this book, along with the free worksheets we provide at http://breakingtape.com/worksheets.html will guide you as you apply the WINNING Method to create your personal plan and achieve the work and life successes you desire.

Part One: Introduction and Overview

- *Introduction & Principles*—Introduces you to the WINNING Method and the guiding principles on which it is based.
- *Overview of the WINNING Method*—Prepares you for your journey.

Part Two: Using the WINNING Method

- *Step 1: **WISH**, then Define Success*—Guides you as you envision and define the success you want in your life.

- *Step 2: **INTERVIEW** a Role Model*—Helps you identify a role model who has already attained the kind of success you want, and gives you tools and tips for interviewing and learning from that person as you build your plan for success.

- *Step 3: **NAME** the Outcomes that Matter*—Helps you understand how outcomes differ from goals, and walks you through the process of defining the outcomes that matter to your plan for success. This is a key differentiator of the WINNING Method compared to approaches that are purely goal-based.

- *Step 4: **NOTE** Success Drivers and Roadblocks*—Presents four key drivers to help you unlock the full power of your plan and teaches you how to identify them. Walks you through the process of identifying the barriers in your life (and at work) that can interfere with your success, and helps you minimize or eliminate them.

- *Step 5: **IDENTIFY** and Measure the Gap*—Examines the gap between your current reality and your desired outcomes to enable you to build a strong foundation for practical goal setting and a clear measure later to see how well your plan worked. Helps you create manageable steps toward your success.

- *Step 6: **NAVIGATE** to Success with Goals*—Introduces you to our BREAK-through goal strategy, a better way to set goals that you can achieve. Guides you through setting the right goals, strategies, and tactics to produce your outcomes. Takes a deeper look at your mindset and approach to success, and how that impacts your goals. Helps you understand what motivates you to make a lasting change. (This will be a critical chapter for many of you because your mind can overrun even your best-laid plans for success.)

- *Step 7: **GAUGE** Progress at Checkpoints*—Teaches you how to define, set, and use checkpoints to monitor, track, and log your progress. Prompts you to celebrate improvements and create long-term, positive habits for life.

As we guide you through the completion of the seven critical steps in the WINNING Method, the threads of success will be woven into the fabric of your personal plan for breaking tape, making the journey easier for you.

Part Three: Extending Your Success

- *Where Do You Go From Here?*— Gives you the opportunity to revisit, refine, or revise your outcomes and goals, learn from your experience to keep yourself motivated, and identify the need for new outcomes.

- *Becoming a Role Model for Others*—Encourages you to reach out and become a role model for those around you, extending your success by giving back. This will be very rewarding to you, personally, and valuable to others starting the journey toward the success they desire.

Why We Wrote This Book

We wrote this book to add greater value to peoples' lives through a deeper understanding of the success they want, and how to attain it at work and home. In this book we share the WINNNG Method with you, enabling you to create and use your personal plan to break tape and achieve your success. The WINNING Method is a structured methodology of best practices for achieving success, and includes a set of worksheets that walk you through each step. (You can download a free PDF of the worksheets you will use to create your Personal Plan for Breaking Tape from our website: http://breakingtape.com/worksheets.html).

Many self-help books operate on a simple goal-based premise. The WINNING Method is different. Goals are a *part* of your plan, but not the *starting point*. Success as you define it is much more than your ability to meet goals. It is your ability to produce the *results you want in the shortest amount of time, and with the fewest setbacks or mistakes*. In other words, you achieve success by accomplishing important things in your life as fast, and as easily as possible. With so much on our plates these days, being effective and efficient means we have to invest less of our precious time and energy to get the results we want.

How Do We Know It Will Work for You?

How do we know the WINNING Method can work for you? Here are three important reasons:

1. **Tested Process.** The concepts and structure behind this approach come from the world of human performance improvement (HPI), a tested process that has been used successfully to assist people and business organizations for over 50 years. We have applied these principles effectively over the last 30 years to help businesses improve their results. We have taken what we learned from this experience to create the WINNING Method, a systematic, holistic process to help you define, plan, and achieve personal and professional success.

2. **Not Focused on Behavior.** Many approaches to achieving personal success focus too much on individual behaviors and actions, rather than on outcomes and results. For example, you make resolutions such as "I will go to the gym," "I will eat leafy greens," or "I will lobby for that promotion." But not all behaviors are equally important, nor will they always drive the results you want in the shortest amount of time, with the fewest costs or missteps.

3. **Personalized**. It is *not a* "one-pill-for-all" process. The WINNING Method guides you as you create a personalized plan for success. It is uniquely focused on *you*—the results *you* want, the role model *you* choose, the outcomes *you* define and the goals *you* set, bounded by the realities within which *you* work.

How Does the WINNING Method Drive Success?

Right now you may be thinking, "How do I know that this method will drive my success?" That's a valid question to ask, because you probably don't have time and energy to invest in a process that is not well grounded.

The WINNING Method will improve your ability to attain the success you want because it is based on four important principles that drive achievement and success. (A *principle* is a fundamental truth that serves as the foundation or core of a system or process.)

Principle 1: Role models help you define the outcomes you need to produce.

Find someone in your workplace or circle of friends who is demonstrating the success you want to achieve. How do you know they are succeeding? What results are they producing? What measures tell you these results are good? The WINNING Method asks you to identify a role model who can help you define the success you want to achieve—and do so in a way that is results-based, feasible, and within your ethical and moral boundaries. This is much easier and less error-prone than trying to create success from scratch, without something to guide you.

Principle 2: Focus first on the results—the outcomes you want to achieve within this system—and only then on goals.

This principle keeps it real. The WINNING Method focuses you first on the outcomes (i.e., the results) that must be achieved. We use the word outcomes in our seven-step method because the term means the "valuable, measurable results you produce." Focusing on outcomes will help you clearly define the end state you want to achieve. This enables you to specify what success looks like—and the outcomes you must produce to achieve it. Only after you define outcomes will you set goals to make your outcomes a reality.

Principle 3: You work and live within a system of success drivers and roadblocks.

You don't operate in a vacuum. Your personal and professional activities all occur within a system. You go to work every day and attempt to produce the results your job requires. But sometimes the things in that system—the tools, resources, technologies, other people, management, noise, motivators, or lack of training—get in the way of your success. The same is true in our lives at home. It is futile to set goals without understanding the system that operates in your home life and how it affects you both positively and negatively. The WINNING Method helps you identify and leverage the success drivers that will help you succeed. It also helps you identify and eliminate the roadblocks that challenge your success. This is an important piece of the success puzzle. The WINNING Method helps you acknowledge the positive and negative influences that affect your ability to accomplish what you want.

Principle 4: Long-term success requires strong belief, emotional maturity, and personal motivation.

The WINNING Method includes numerous opportunities for you to explore and activate the emotional and motivational factors that will help you achieve and maintain success. These include the belief that change for the better is possible and within your reach, the emotional maturity to persevere every day until you achieve success, and your ability to tap into what motivates you.

Closing Thoughts

We created the WINNING Method based on these four principles to help you achieve success faster and smarter, and to keep your work and home life in balance—something we all are challenged to do every day. Learning from your role models saves you time and energy. Focusing on the outcomes that drive the success you want minimizes the risk of failure and enables you to try something different with a great sense of confidence. Understanding the system within which you work and live helps you plan your approach, work through roadblocks, and keeps you motivated. Finally, developing and using your belief in yourself, applying emotional maturity to the process, and activating your motivating factors ensures that you continue moving forward, doing what is needed every day to attain your successes!

Think this all sounds simple? It is. But it takes structure and guidance to get it right and stay the course, a WINNING Method you can easily apply, and a commitment to practice and follow through. If you want to achieve any kind of success, you must be willing to focus your efforts, experiment with an open mind, try (and sometimes fail), learn from the outcome, and try again.

The next chapter gives you an overview of the WINNING Method and summarizes the seven steps you will be taking toward the success you desire.

Overview of the WINNING Method

"Every great accomplishment, every desire, started as a wish with a plan." – Karen McGraw

The WINNING Method is a seven-step technique or process to help you create and apply a well-developed plan for success. We use the word WINNING as an acronym that defines the key components of your plan for success. As you break tape with our WINNING Method, you are not racing against others; you are running your own race, toward something *you* want to accomplish.

Have you ever been passionate about learning something? Do you remember when you first learned to ride a bicycle? Maybe some of your friends were already riding their bikes without training wheels; you were determined to do the same. You could see yourself riding down the road right next to your friends, taking off to places unknown or that were once out of reach. Everything that happened in that experience, from having the wish or desire to ride that bike and talking to your friends about how it was done, to determinedly modeling their behavior, enabled you to accomplish your wish and succeed. There is something quite simple and direct about our early wins, but somehow many of us fail to apply that directness to our grown-up selves. The pure essence of these early winning experiences can be transferred to help us achieve what we want to accomplish today. In this book, we help you apply our WINNING Method both at work and in your personal life, to achieve your goals and desires.

We named the book and the results it produces "breaking tape" because the method is much like a marathon runner breaking the tape at the finish line. That runner is running with a goal in mind—a best time to accomplish, or that incredible feeling of finishing all 42.195 kilometers (26 miles and 385 yards). In the end, a marathon runner is not racing against others. Many will tell you that they are racing against themselves and their very understandable desire to quit. They race for their wish to succeed and their definition of success.

Most successful runners have a winning method or approach that helps get them to the finish line. Similarly, when we analyze high performers or very successful people, we find that they also have a specific approach they apply to help them achieve success, over and over again. We have taken that concept of "breaking tape" and paired it with the WINNING Method—an approach or technique that helps you get to the finish line for your success. It makes no difference if you are applying this WINNING Method to attaining financial freedom in your life, losing weight, managing a huge project, or getting that promotion at work. There is some sort of

WINNING Method that is used to achieve these successes, whether you are conscious of it or not.

We all need a WINNING Method in our lives. Simply wishing for your dream of personal or professional success isn't enough. It never is. (It wouldn't have helped you ride that bicycle, either!) Having a WINNING Method—a proven process with worksheets that guide you each step of the way—greatly improves your chances of success!

Steps in the WINNING Method

In this book you will learn how to apply the WINNING Method, bringing the success you want to achieve to life, and breaking tape in your work and/or personal life. Like a successful long-distance runner who prepares for a race, this will require multiple steps and layers of activities. Figure 1 illustrates the major steps you will take to craft your personal plan for success and put it to work for you. Let's walk through them together at a high level. In other chapters of this book we will give you all the details and pointers to the worksheets you will need to complete each step with confidence and ease.

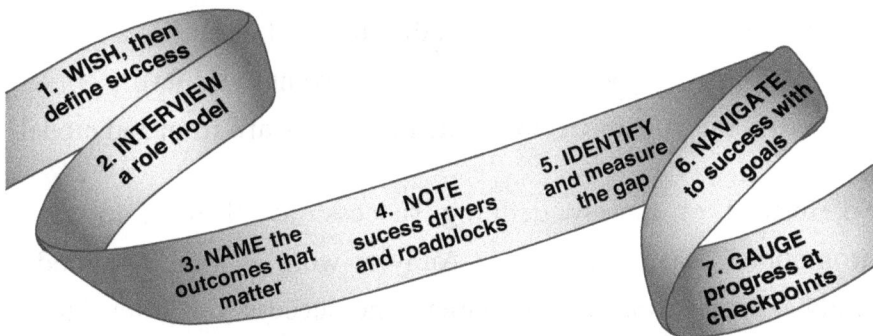

1. WISH, then define success
2. INTERVIEW a role model
3. NAME the outcomes that matter
4. NOTE sucess drivers and roadblocks
5. IDENTIFY and measure the gap
6. NAVIGATE to success with goals
7. GAUGE progress at checkpoints

Figure 1. The seven-step WINNING Method to Break Tape

STEP 1 helps you begin with the end in mind as you create your **wish that defines success,** asking questions such as:

- What *type* of success am I trying to achieve at work or in my personal life?
- How do I define success in this area of my life?
- What are the criteria that I will use to measure my success?

This is an important first step. If the success you want is not well-defined, how will you know when you've attained it? To paraphrase the Cheshire Cat in Lewis Carroll's *Alice in Wonderland*, if you don't know where you are going, any road will get you there eventually—if you walk long enough. Many of us wander aimlessly toward success, setting goals without really understanding the end state we want to achieve. This step helps you clearly define your destination and dream, making it easier to set a visible path forward. Remember a wish is simply a vision of your success with a due date tied to its completion. Getting there takes applying the rest of the steps in the WINNING Method.

STEP 2 helps you keep it real as you **interview a role model.** To find your role model you will ask:

- Who has already attained the success I desire?
- Who is a good example of what I want to achieve?
- Is this role model available for me to learn from and model?

So, instead of loosely defining success, as "I want to get a promotion," you decide to use Andy at work as your role model. Andy not only was able to achieve the success you want, but he did so without sacrificing his marriage or family relationships. His ability to maintain family relationships is a critical component of his success, and this is a moral or ethical value that is important to you, as well. In Andy, you have a practical, positive model who will help you achieve the kind of success you want faster than you could on your own, and without unintended consequences. Better yet, by identifying someone who has already attained the success you desire, you don't have to reinvent the wheel to discover how to achieve it yourself. And you won't have to wonder if the success you want is attainable. Your role model has demonstrated that it can be achieved.

STEP 3 guides you as you **name the outcomes that matter** to attain the success you want. An outcome is

- The valuable end result of something you do, or
- Something important you leave behind or produce as a result of something you do.

Outcomes are stated in positive words to help you make the outcome tangible and fuel your success. For example, many of us want to lose weight or get ourselves in better shape. A positive, tangible outcome for this desired state might be: "I am 20 pounds lighter and have established healthy eating and exercise habits." Setting a positive outcome helps you focus on the results you must produce to achieve the success you desire. Outcomes will drive our results and lead us toward success.

STEP 4 requires you to think about the system in which you live and work and how it helps or hinders your success. For our purposes, a system is made up of the many influences and relationships that together, create the entire picture of your situation. In Step 4, you will **note the success drivers and roadblocks** that either support or hinder your success. What are the success drivers that will help you break your tape and achieve success? Similarly, what are the roadblocks that may be getting in the way of your success?

A system exists in an environment—your work, or your home, for example. At work, your system includes components such as the following:

- How your job is defined
- The processes you must use to do your work
- The computer applications that help you do your work
- Your manager
- Your work team
- Outside influences impacting your ability to do something.

At home, your system may include components such as the individual relationships among family members, your "home rules," your resources (such as money and time), and how things get done around your house.

In this step we introduce you to four important success drivers and the roadblocks that may get in the way of your success. We ask you to examine your work or home system to identify the drivers in your life that will help you achieve the success you desire. We also ask you to anticipate likely roadblocks to success and define what you will do about each one. Having a plan that addresses both drivers and roadblocks will increase your ability to break tape and achieve your desired success.

STEP 5 in the development of your plan is a gap analysis. You need to **identify and measure the gap** between where you are today (in terms of achieving your work or life success) versus where you want to be. In business, gap analysis is a tool that helps organizations compare *actual* performance with *desired* performance. But you can use gap analysis, too, simply by comparing where you are now, with something you desire in your future.

Asking questions such as these will help you gain a better understanding of the gap and how to close it:

- Where am I today in terms of the success I wish and envision?
- Where do I want to be?
- How best can I use my capabilities and resources to achieve success?

This step builds on each of the outcomes you have identified to determine, "how far am I today from being able to produce this outcome?" You will identify and measure the gap, then check yourself to make sure that closing the gap is feasible.

STEP 6 of the WINNING Method requires you to **navigate to success with goals** by defining measurable goals for each outcome. When attained, these goals should close the gaps you identified in Step 5, enabling you to produce your desired outcomes and break tape. We help you set what we call BREAK-through (Believable, Realistic, Explicit, Activate your drive, and Key measures) goals, a powerful, simple process to establish and measure a set of actions to achieve your goals. Think back to our weight loss example from Step 3. Your gap today is 20 pounds. Some examples of BREAK-through goals that could be set to close the gap and achieve this outcome might be:

- Plan and cook healthy, low-fat dinners at least five times a week for the next 16 weeks.
- Complete 45 minutes of aerobic exercise and 30 minutes of yoga at least three times a week for the next 16 weeks.

Once you have identified BREAK-through goals to close the gap, you will document the strategies and tactics you will use to meet each goal. A strategy refers to a direction toward your goal, while tactics are specific actions you take to support the strategy.

One critical strategy in our WINNING Method and your plan for success is your approach and mindset, including how you will approach each goal. Through this process you may discover that the approach you have used in the past is vastly different from the approach your role model shared with you. For example, your role model may have had success exercising at a set time in the early morning. In contrast, you exercise at the end of the day, raising the odds that you would not do it. Changing your approach to meet your goal could make all the difference in achieving it!

Additionally, your strategy and tactics must include your motivation to achieve each goal. What motivates you to attain the goals you have set? What is going to keep you motivated every day? Many people find that they must change their mindset and tweak their motivation to break the tape on their success.

Step 7 will help you **gauge your progress at checkpoints** by monitoring, measuring, and documenting your progress and achievement. The goals that you set in Step 6 are like the rudder of a boat. They will help keep you on course, moving toward the success you have envisioned. A good sailor constantly monitors progress toward his destination. This constant, real-time measurement is what this step is all about. It enables our sailor to make the slight adjustments needed, when they are needed, to keep the boat on course. It is much easier (and safer) to monitor and gauge the boat's progress and make slight adjustments routinely, than to make over-corrections or abandon ship later.

In this step you will set checkpoints for each goal and determine measures that let you look critically at your progress. Like a good sailor, you can then make the adjustments your plan needs to continually help you move toward the finish line and the success you desire. And as your success becomes a reality, you celebrate your achievement and use it to create long-term, positive habits for life.

Closing Thoughts

We've introduced you to the WINNING Method and provided you with an overview of the steps you will take to break tape on the success you desire. Are you still doubtful because you've tried other self-help methods and not achieved the results you desired?

Remember, the WINNING Method is a proven, research-based process to help you achieve the success you want. It includes structured steps to guide you and the practical tools and worksheets you'll need to create and commit to your plan for breaking tape on the success you desire! We have tested and tried these techniques and processes many times, all over the world, with great success. You are not the first person to use them to create change in your life!

We suspect that because you are reading this book, you want something more or different in your life. We're looking forward to sharing with you how to make your desired success a reality. Let's get started—let your journey begin now!

PART TWO

Using the WINNING Method

Step 1: WISH, then Define Success

Step 2: INTERVIEW a Role Model

Step 3: NAME the Outcomes that Matter

Step 4: NOTE Success Drivers and Roadblocks

Step 5: IDENTIFY and Measure the Gap

Step 6: NAVIGATE to Success with Goals

Step 7: GAUGE Progress at Checkpoints

STEP 1

WISH, then Define Success

"Envisioning success brings you an inspiring image, but bringing that image to life requires action." – Larina Kase, psychologist

Every winner in any sport, or in any workplace, creates a vision of what success will look like. This is a fundamental truth for anyone who is highly successful. That vision is then refined through discussions with others in their field or sport and reflections on lessons learned from other successful people. The clearer the vision, the more complete the picture of success becomes, and the higher the chances that this person gets what they want. The personal plan you will create using our WINNING Method is no exception.

In this chapter you will craft a vision of what you want both personally and/or professionally, refine it, and commit to your vision. This process will result in a firm foundation for breaking tape. You will build on this foundation for success as you complete subsequent chapters and develop your personal plan for achieving the success you desire.

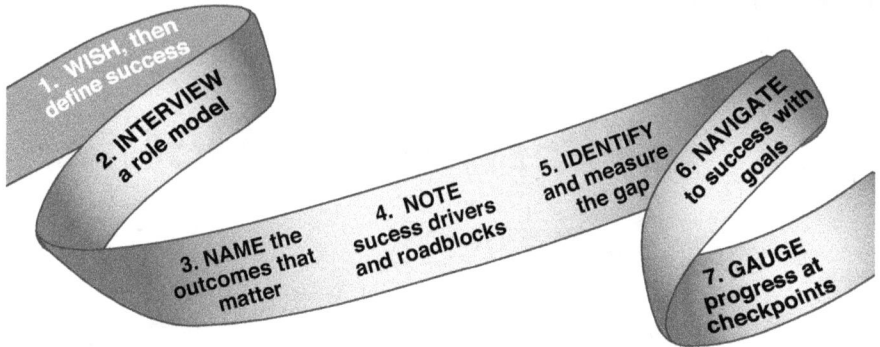

Figure 2. You are on your way!

You probably have a rough idea of the success you would like to achieve. Now you need to explore it more deeply, let yourself believe in your success, and begin the process of making it a reality.

Believe. It's a simple word that means to accept something as true, or to feel sure of something. For many people, it is also the missing piece in achieving the success they want. If you don't believe your success is possible, it probably won't be. Maybe you remember the children's book, *The Little Engine that Could*, by Watty Piper. The book tells the story of a little train engine that attained a very difficult goal with hard work and a persistent belief in success. The little engine's motto, "I think I can, I think I can," became the fuel for success. Believing you can attain the success you desire goes hand-in-hand with the hard work you do to make it a reality.

A psychologist at Stanford University, Albert Bandura, researched why believing in yourself and your dreams has such an impact on whether or not you will be successful in life. His research concluded that believing in oneself is the first step to being successful. In other words, simply setting goals and making plans is futile if we don't believe we can attain them. He also determined that we are not born with this trait. Our experience working with people at all levels in companies across America supports Bandura's theory. Believing in ourselves is something that we all have to learn to incorporate in our lives if we want to achieve the success we desire.

The goal of this chapter is to help you envision the success you want and make it seem tangible by defining it as a clear wish that you believe you can achieve.

We will guide you through the steps you need to take to meet this goal. You will document and commit to your vision for success, using the tools in this chapter and available online. By the end of this chapter you will have a stronger, believable success vision that is within your reach, and to which you want to commit your time and energy to accomplish. This well-documented wish will be the start of your personal plan for breaking tape.

Don't skip this step! The result—a firm foundation for breaking tape! Without a firm foundation, your wish will not be on solid ground. This step is worth it.

Get Real by Envisioning Your Wish, then Define Success

You are the architect of your success. You have chosen to take one or more parts of your life to the next level. Right now, the success you want may look a bit fuzzy; the vision may not be totally clear. This is all right for the moment, but it will not work over the long term. If you are not completely clear about what you want, you are less likely to achieve it.

That's why our WINNING Method starts with a validated **process** to help you define your wish in a tangible way, for the long term. The more clearly you envision the success you desire as your wish, the more real it becomes to you. The more real it becomes to you, the greater your belief that you can attain it. The greater the belief in your wish, the higher the likelihood that you will achieve the results you desire (Figure 3).

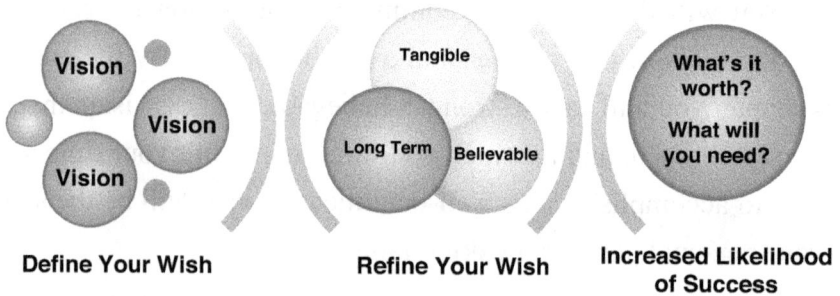

Vision

Vision

Vision

Define Your Wish

Tangible

Long Term   Believable

Refine Your Wish

What's it worth?

What will you need?

Increased Likelihood of Success

Figure 3. Increasing the likelihood of success starts with defining and refining your wish

The process for envisioning success and defining your wish is called *visualization*. It has been used by many people to get real about what they want. It works because by visualizing the end result, you become more motivated to achieve it, and your mind is more likely to help you move toward your vision.

How Do you Visualize Success to Define your Wish?

The process for visualizing success to define your wish isn't hard, but it does require that you set aside 20-30 minutes to complete the process. Additionally, find a time and a quiet place that will allow you to complete the process undisturbed. During this process you are asking your mind to daydream, think about, and envision success as you begin to define your wish. If your mind begins to wander onto other topics, just gently refocus it on the wish or success you want.

We recommend that you identify no more than one or two success visions or wishes. Target those things that you are aching to change in your life right away. For example, you want to improve your health at the same time that you wish to build or deepen relationships with friends or family. The reason we suggest focusing on one or two success visions at a time is that it can be overwhelming and often self-defeating to define more than one or two wishes at a time. You can always repeat this process after you have attained the one or two wishes that are most important to you at this time.

Follow the steps we provide in the next few pages to visualize success and define your wish. The *Wish, then Define Success Worksheet* will guide you in creating and documenting your vision. (A free PDF of all of the worksheets you will use throughout the WINNING Method to complete your personal plan for breaking tape is available for download at http://breakingtape.com/worksheets.html.)

Before you begin, choose a quiet place. Visualization will only work when you are calm and willing to give yourself time to focus. Watch your intake of caffeine or other stimulants, because they can get in the way of your ability to relax and focus.

1. **Write this question** on a piece of paper, in a digital document, or on a whiteboard: "What kind of success do I desire?"
   o *Tip*: Remember, your wish for success can be about work, home, your relationships with others, your health, or anything else important to you.

2. **Look at this question in a very focused way**. Let yourself daydream as you begin to think about your answer. Expect your creative mind to take the lead in helping you imagine what it would be like after you have made your wish a reality.
   o *Tip*: As answers come to mind, jot these ideas down on the worksheet or a notepad.

3. **Make your wish long-term**. You know the change won't happen overnight. For example, it's unlikely you will become a vice president next year if you are in a first-level management position today.
   o Visualize where you will be in two years, and in five years, including how your life will be better after making this change. Ask yourself what legacies you want to leave behind for your family, your friends, and your community.
   o How will others around you be better off?

- o   How will you feel or think about yourself?
- o   How will others view you?
- o   Take a moment to record these thoughts about long-term success.

4. **Document your belief in your wish** and commit to it.
    - o   Think about why you believe your vision of success is possible.
    - o   Get specific and write one or more belief statements to bolster your commitment to your wish.
    - o   Later, as you define outcomes and begin to set goals, (something you will learn more about in the coming chapters) you will return to these belief statements to help you stay motivated.

5. **Ask yourself what you will need to be successful on this journey.**
    - o   Think back on the mental images that came to mind when you visualized your success.
    - o   What will you need to make these images a reality? For example, "I need to find reliable child care," "I need to go back to school," or "I need to acquire a laptop computer."
    - o   *Tip*: Don't get too deep here, just look for the basics that you will need and jot them down.

6. **Think about what this wish is worth to you**. Document what you are willing to do to make it a reality.
    - o   *Note*: Giving the wish worth will help you commit to it more strongly.
    - o   Confirm your desire to achieve this wish.

Use the *Wish, then Define Success Worksheet* (Parts 1 and 2) in the worksheet PDF packet http://breakingtape.com/worksheets.html as you create your success vision and record your wish. (See Figures 4 and 5 for snapshots of this worksheet.) Recording your wish helps you make it real, transferring it from your imagination to the written word.

A funny thing happens to most people when they commit to something in writing. They are more likely to make it happen! If you want to improve the likelihood of achieving your wish, share it with a few people you trust and respect. These people can encourage you to make your wish a reality. Ask them for their support as you move through the WINNING Method. They are most likely not going to be your coaches in this journey, but friends and colleagues who can push and encourage you from time to time.

Wish, then Define Success Worksheet, Part 1 ***Visualize your Wish and Describe Success***	
Guiding Question	**Response**
1. Describe your wish for success in broad terms. *Examples: I want to start my own business. I want to move from a technical position to the supervisory ladder and become a manager at work. I want my family to be happy and successful. I want a closer, more loving relationship with my spouse. I want to improve my health and wellbeing.*	
2. Visualize what it will be like once you have made this wish a reality. What words come to mind to describe what this success will be like? (*Write down as many words as come into your mind, as quickly as you can. There is no right or wrong here. Write what you discover.*)	

3. When your wish becomes real, certain things in your life will change, or be different. What will success look like in the future? Be as specific as you can by answering the questions provided for each time period:

In two years	In five years
How will my life be better after making this wish real?	How will my life be better after making this wish real?
How will others around me be better off?	How will others around me be better off?
How will I feel or think about myself?	How will I feel or think about myself?
How will others (friend, spouse, child, co-worker, boss, etc.) view me?	How will others (friend, spouse, child, co-worker, boss, etc.) view me?

Figure 4. Snapshot of Part 1 of the Wish, then Define Success Worksheet

Wish, then Define Success Worksheet, Part 2
Enabling the Vision
4. With your success wish clear in your mind, can you commit to it? What makes you believe it is possible to make this change happen? Write one or two belief statements here:
5. What will I need to be successful on this journey? Think back on the mental images that came to mind when you visualized your success wish. What do you think you will need to make those images a reality? (Note: Do not get yourself in too deep here. Look for the basics and the obvious things that you will need.) I will need the following basic things to make this success wish a reality:
6. What is it worth to you to achieve this success wish? What are you willing to sacrifice or give up (e.g., time, freedom, anxiety, cost of doing something to attain new skills, etc.) to make this vision a reality? To make this success wish a reality, I am willing to sacrifice or give up:

Figure 5. Snapshot of Part 2 of the Wish, then Define Success Worksheet

The completed worksheets will become tools you use to you refocus and recalibrate yourself later, should you get off track.

Closing Thoughts

Congratulations! You have just documented and committed to the success wish you have envisioned. You have finished the first step in the WINNING Method and started creating your personal plan for breaking tape and achieving the success you deserve!

This chapter guided you through a very important front-end process that traditional goal books overlook. *We know that envisioning your wish and defining the success you desire, keeping it real, and believing and committing to it greatly improves your chances of attaining it.*

Every successful person must get clear on how they define success. Now you, too, have a rich vision of the success you want to create—your wish.

You will use your wish and the worksheets you have completed as you take the next step in the WINNING Method—select and interview a role model. We recommend that you write your wish on an index card and post it where you can see it daily. Print the completed worksheets and store them close at hand for quick reference. These steps will make it easier for you to reflect on your wish as you interview your role model and create the different components (gaps, outcomes, goals, etc.) that will comprise your personal plan for breaking tape.

Motivational Checkpoint

1. What is the main reason you want to achieve the success wish you have envisioned and documented?

2. How can you motivate yourself to keep this wish alive as you begin this journey?

3. What close friends or colleagues do you want in your inner circle to champion and support your wish as you begin this journey?

Work it Out

Apply the concepts and steps described in this chapter to complete this section of your personal plan for breaking tape. For ease of use, please download a PDF containing all of the worksheets you need to construct your Personal Plan for Breaking Tape from our website: http://breakingtape.com/worksheets.html.

Wish, then Define Success Worksheet

Directions: Respond to the questions to complete Parts 1 and 2 of the worksheet.

STEP 2

INTERVIEW a Role Model

"I take as much as advice and inspiration as I can from the people I am close to." – Natalie Massenet, American entrepreneur

When we begin to plan how we will achieve the success we want, we often make the mistake of jumping right in and going it alone. We get excited about getting started. We don't want to take the time to see if someone else has done it, and how they did so. Or maybe our ego gets in the way of asking for help.

Someone (and probably someone you know) has already attained the wish you want to achieve. Who are they? Have they achieved it in the way you want to? What can you learn from them to help you on your journey?

Caution: If you fail to seek out and learn from others who have tackled achievements similar to your wish, you waste time and energy. Instead, we suggest you reach out to someone who has achieved something similar to your wish and definition of success. Find out how he or she did it and what helped. Along the way you might also learn what *not* to do, and how to recover from common roadblocks to your success. These bits of knowledge enable you to build on the success of others and help keep you motivated on your journey.

We use the term "role model" to describe someone in your workplace, your neighborhood, or circle of friends who can serve as an example, and from whom you can learn. After all, you probably are not the first person who has wanted to achieve the type of success wish you envision, so why go it alone? Why make mistakes when you don't need to?

The goals of this chapter are to help you

- Identify a role model
- Interview your role model to capture lessons learned to help you achieve your vision.

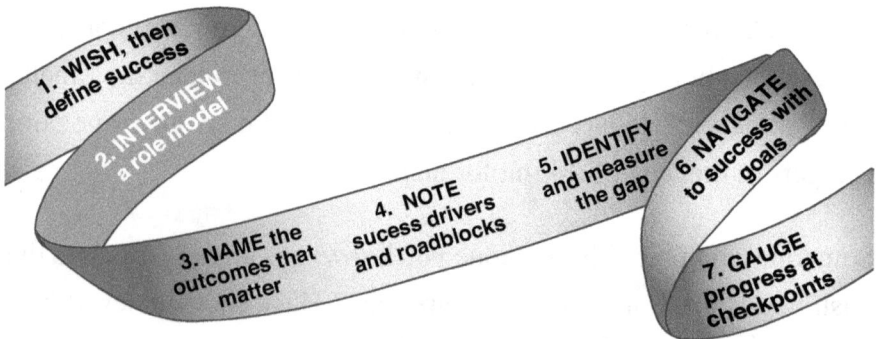

Figure 6. Ready for Step 2

To accomplish these goals, you will use the following tools: a checklist (to choose your role model) and a worksheet (to interview that person). Both tools are included in the PDF worksheet packet.

You will use the completed *Role Model Interview Worksheet* to fine-tune your wish, and as a starting point to consider the outcomes you must be able to produce to achieve the wish. By the end of this chapter, you will have captured lessons learned or tips for achieving your wish. You can use these lessons and tips to refine your success wish, if necessary, and to make your commitment to your wish more real.

Don't skip this step! The foundation for your personal plan for breaking tape will be even stronger.

Choose a Role Model for Success

When we were growing up, we looked to role models for inspiration and guidance for how to behave. Whether they were our parents or other adults, or someone else we aspired to be like, we learned from these role models. We may have learned how to be successful and happy people. We may have learned how to respond and recover when bad things happen. And we may have learned what *not* to do. Having the right role models probably made it easier for some of us to grow up and take on the challenges of adult life at work and at home.

As adults, we still need role models in our lives. In the WINNING Method, these role models become our models for success. Just as we learned from role models during our childhood, so too can we learn from them as adults. However, having the right role model is critical. (Or as Karen often told her children, "Show me your friends, and I'll show you your future".)

Your role models are real, living, breathing people you can observe and with whom you can interact. They are important and unique for you; they have already achieved the success you want. They may have made the transition from worker to manager, or from being unhealthy to having healthy living habits. They have demonstrated that the wish you desire is possible. These role models often live and work right around you, making them easy to find. Some of the things role models can share with you include:

- How they approached the transition from A to B (e.g., being unhealthy to being healthy)
- What new skills they needed to succeed, and how they obtained them
- What sort of knowledge they already had, or gained in the process of achieving their wish
- What difficulties they faced and how they approached and overcame them
- What they learned from failures along the way
- How they measured their progress
- What kept them motivated to make the change and achieve success
- Tips for making the transition you have visualized.

Most importantly, because your role model has already figured out what it takes to achieve something similar to your success wish, you can learn from them. They keep you from reinventing the wheel, or trying something that won't work. As a result, they save you time and energy, which increases your chances of achieving the success you desire.

Finding and Selecting a Role Model

Role models are all around you; at work, in the neighborhood, at church or the synagogue, at the gym, and at your kids' sporting events or school.

Choosing your role model is more difficult than finding one. First, be honest with yourself—do you know what you want from your role model? Do you want a quick conversation about how they attained the success you want? Or, do you want to find someone you can meet with initially, but check back with for short, periodic conversations? Many people might be willing to share ideas with you to help you get started and avoid their missteps, while fewer will be interested in meeting with you over a longer term. The latter might prove to be more valuable and useful at other stages on your journey to breaking tape.

What we are suggesting is different from having a formal, defined relationship with a mentor at work. Mentors have to commit time to you, and you to them, over a long period. Most of us won't be able to find someone with this sort of time to give. Instead, the WINNING Method will guide you through the process of

Asking the right questions,
      Of the right person (your role model),
            To gain a picture of all the right stuff you will need to learn, do, change, and adapt to achieve your success wish.

It is a technique we have used and tested for many years in organizations all over the world, as well as with family members, friends, and ourselves.

One important key is to identify people in your world who are currently living and openly demonstrating the success you envision and the wish you defined. It is the little details that will make a difference, so look very carefully at the total package before you choose. In other words, if you seek a balanced approach to your life along with the promotion you want, you would not choose the hard-charging executive who was successful and received promotions but whose marriage fell apart on the way to the top. Similarly, if you have strong moral positions, you would not choose the success-at-all-costs person. You choose your role model based on the success you have envisioned, supported by your personal values and moral compass. If these get too much out of alignment, you will not be happy with the result.

The PDF worksheet packet includes a checklist to help you select your role model. Figure 7 illustrates a snapshot of this checklist. If you have several potential role models for the success you have envisioned, duplicate the checklist and complete one for each, to help you select the *best* model.

Checklist for Selecting a Role Model
Name of the Potential Role Model:
1. **Successful in your eyes**—has attained the measure of success you want, and also is the kind of person you want to be (aligned with your morals/values)   *Notes:*
2. **Consistently successful**—has demonstrated the success wish you have defined, over time   *Notes:*
3. **Willing to be honest**—is willing to give you honest input on how realistic your success wish is and what exactly it takes to achieve it   *Notes:*
4. **Open and transparent**—is willing to share not only what has worked but also what has not worked   *Notes:*
5. **Available for the interview**—is not so busy that it would be difficult to meet with you for 30-45 minutes and answer your questions   *Notes:*
6. **Can be supportive of your journey** —is willing to offer motivational support to help you accomplish your success wish   *Notes:*

Figure 7. Snapshot of the Checklist for Selecting a Role Model

Using the completed checklist(s), select the person you would ideally like to be your role model. It is possible that you will not have ✓ s in all six areas for every potential model. The goal is to find a balance of ✓ s in the areas that are critical to you, and to select a primary role model (and possibly, a secondary role model who can be a backup, if needed). It is possible that you could end up with a few role models, though more than two would be unusual.

Getting Buy-In from Your Role Model

You have selected someone as your primary role model (and possibly another person as a backup). Now it's time to ask your preferred role model to help you by sharing his/her experience.

Approach your role model and share the success wish you have envisioned. Tell them you would like them to serve as your model for the success you'd like to achieve. Be prepared to describe what you are asking them to do. For example, at a minimum, you need them to meet with you for 30-45 minutes to share how they achieved the success you desire, and what worked for them. To do so, you will be asking them some simple questions to answer from their personal experience. (The *Role Model Interview Worksheet* presented later in this chapter provides questions and advice on what to look for, so you won't feel uncomfortable completing this step.)

If you know the person well, and you know that you might need more of their input over time, you can ask them to meet with you once a month for a set period. This could be very helpful, especially if you hit some bumps during your journey or need a little extra motivational push. If you're like many people, you start out with great intentions and plans, but lack the drive and motivation to make it happen over the long haul. In this case, it will be very beneficial to have a role model who can champion your vision and remind and encourage you along the way.

Set the meeting with your role model for as soon as possible, but at a minimum within the next week. This will help ensure that you do not lose momentum and can keep your success wish fresh. Ask for a specific date and time, and commit to making it happen. Put this meeting date on your calendar and remember that this is an important appointment. Treat it like other important appointments for which you have set aside time. Right now, you and your desired success are just as important—and maybe more so—than other appointments you have set.

Conducting the Meeting with Your Role Model

Prepare for the meeting with your role model by imagining that you are a great detective (Figure 8). Your job is to ask good questions, listen actively, and discover what is working for this person. You will be listening not only for what is said, but also for what is not said. Body language that indicates there is something more to be said (e.g., a finger against lips), for example, requires that you follow up with, "Is there something else you're thinking about that might be helpful?" Or, body language such as placing arms protectively across the chest may indicate reluctance to share a failure. But remember—it is just as important to understand what did not work for a person, and how they recovered from failures or roadblocks leading to their success. These will be important to know later when you encounter challenges.

If you don't already have experience using active listening, we suggest that you practice it before you meet with your role model. You can practice while watching a TV program, listening to a radio talk show, or simply by sitting in a coffee shop where you can hear people talking.

The key is to capture exactly what someone says and write this down without changing what they say or interpreting it. To do this correctly, you must turn off the noise in your head and your pre-conceived notions of what is 'right' or 'wrong.' Just listen without judgment to what is being said. It sounds easy, but it takes a little practice to get good at it.

Figure 8. Be a good "success" detective

When the meeting with your role model occurs, kick it off by thanking them for their time and willingness to be candid in their responses to your questions. Briefly share your vision for the success you desire. Remind them why you chose them as your role model. Then tell them you will be asking questions to better understand how they achieved success.

The *Role Model Interview Worksheet* illustrated in Figure 9 and included in the PDF worksheet packet will help you ask the right questions and capture the main points of their responses.

Role Model Interview Worksheet	
1.	(If you have not already done so, share your success wish.) Then ask: Is my vision of success realistic? What could I do to fine-tune it and make it more realistic?
2.	What path did you take to achieve a similar success? (Said another way: Please tell me what you had to accomplish to achieve your similar success.)
3.	What skills or knowledge did you use to make success a reality for you? What special skills did you have to acquire?
4.	Where or from whom can I get these skills or knowledge?
5.	What are the main things or activities that you had to do in order to achieve this success?"
6.	Was there a time when you struggled or failed along the path to your success? If so, at what point did this happen? How did you get going again?
7.	In your experience, what makes the biggest difference between the people who achieve success and those who don't? (Said another way: Have you seen people who tried but failed to achieve this wish? What caused them to fail or give up?)
8.	What were the critical factors, or things, that you had to attend to, and make sure you did, to achieve your success? (*Note*: A critical factor could be anything that affected their ability to achieve success.)
9.	What were the milestones you used to help make sure you were moving in the right direction? (Said another way: What measures of success did you use to track your progress?)

Figure 9. Snapshot of the Role Model Interview Worksheet

(*Suggestion*: Take a pad of paper, a laptop, or other electronic device with you, in case your role model shares more than you can record on the worksheet.)

Watch your time to ensure you complete your session on time. At the end of the meeting, thank them for their time. Tell them you will be using their responses to help you identify the outcomes you need to produce and the goals you want to achieve to make your vision of success a reality. (We will get into the details of outcomes and goals in the coming chapters.)

Reviewing the Completed Worksheet

The interview with your role model should have provided you with a wealth of information. In a quiet place, within a few hours of the interview, review the notes you compiled. We recommend that your review take place no more than eight hours after the interview because of the limits of short-term memory. Replay the interview in your mind as you review your notes. Look for information to answer the following questions:

- What are the key points my role model shared with me?
- What are the major points I want to make sure to focus on?
- What did I learn that surprised me or was unexpected?
- How will what I learned alter my success wish, or how I want to move forward?

Based on what you have learned, do you need to refine your wish and definition of success to make it more feasible, or to improve your chances of attaining it? If so, take this opportunity to revisit and refine it now, before moving forward.

Closing Thoughts

This chapter guided you through the process of identifying and interviewing a role model to help you learn from his or her experience and fine tune your vision. *Learning from others who have demonstrated the success you desire improves your chances of achieving it yourself.* Like the curing of the foundation for a building, the process of working with a role model helps strengthen your personal plan for breaking tape and completes the second step in the WINNING Method.

You will use the worksheet you completed in this chapter as you begin to identify the outcomes you must be able to produce in order to achieve success (Step 3). Keep it handy for quick reference.

Motivational Checkpoint

1. What do you think is the most important thing you learned so far from the role model with whom you met?

2. How do you see yourself putting into practice some of the tips you learned from your role model?

3. What kind of support would you like to have from your role model moving forward?

4. What are you excited to discover about yourself?

Work it Out

Apply the concepts and steps described in this chapter to complete this section of your personal plan for breaking tape.

Checklist for Selecting a Role Model

Directions: Enter the name of your potential role model in the Checklist. Create a separate sheet for each potential model, but have no more than two models. Then review these items for each model and put a check beside the ones that are true for your potential role model.

Role Model Interview Worksheet

Directions: Ask the questions to get information about how your model achieved the success you desire. Listen carefully and note responses exactly as they are stated. Don't be afraid to ask questions another way if you do not get a useful answer.

STEP 3

NAME the Outcomes that Matter

"Those who speak do not know; those who know do not speak."
– Ancient Taoist saying

Have you noticed? Everyone seems to have an opinion on how you could be more successful. You announce your wish to family and friends, and within no time, they're sharing lots of ideas on how to do it. Why does this happen? Key people in your life care about you and want you to succeed. But unless they have achieved something like your wish and definition of success, their opinion is just that—a personal judgment that may not be very helpful to you.

Instead of listening to every opinion about how to achieve your wish, we ask you to listen to the role model you selected (in Step 2). We want you to hear what your role model believes must be accomplished for you to achieve your success. That person has already produced the real outcomes (i.e., the results) that helped him or her attain the success you want. We want you to benefit from that insight and experience as you create your unique personal plan for breaking tape.

In Step 3 you will observe or interview your role model to understand the outcomes or results that he or she produced on the way to success. Outcomes are critical because they help you break down your definition of success into the individual components that you must be able to produce.

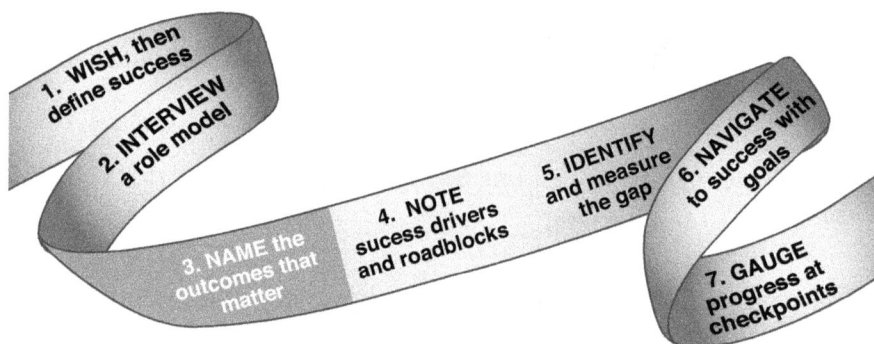

Figure 10. Ready for Step 3

In this chapter we will teach you
- What an outcome is
- Why you should focus on outcomes instead of behaviors
- How to identify outcomes and find the ones that matter
- How to make sure the outcomes are appropriate for you.

What is an Outcome?

In the WINNING Method an outcome is a valuable end result that must be produced by you to achieve the success you desire.

Outcomes are also described as what is created and left behind (i.e., the output) as you meet goals and achieve your wish.

Imagine yourself standing at the edge of a ravine. You know what you want—to get to the other side. You can see it, but it is just out of reach. You could jump, but it might be a painful experience. You could walk for a few miles and maybe find a spot where you could jump safely, but this could take time and energy, if you can find such a spot at all. You can lessen your risk and decrease the time it takes to reach the other side by finding a log (or two) to use as a bridge to cross the ravine. Outcomes are like a bridge between your current reality and your wish or definition of success. Identifying the outcomes successful people produced to attain something similar to your wish gives you a faster path forward, with less risk. Figure 11 illustrates this relationship.

Figure 11. Outcomes are the bridge between your current reality and your wish

Outcomes or Behaviors?

An outcome usually begins with a noun or a noun phrase (e.g., proposal, new sale, client relationship, etc.). It is something that has been produced as the result of a set of behaviors and activities. It is not the set of behaviors and activities themselves, however.

For example, "Client relationship that results in new business and revenue" is an outcome for a sales role. The actions that led to that outcome, such as "calling the client weekly," and "inviting the client to special events" are behaviors. Figure 12 illustrates this difference.

OUTCOMES	BEHAVIORS
Client relationship that results in new business and revenue	• Calling the client weekly to check in • Inviting the client to special events • Writing a good proposal • Identifying new opportunities • Taking my sales manager, an ex-pro football player, with me to see the client • Hustling to respond to any client question
Satisfied hotel guest checked into the hotel	• Looking up a reservation in the computer • Smiling and welcoming the guest • Moving quickly behind the desk • Running the credit card to secure payment • Re-coding the door keys • Asking if they have any questions

Figure 12. Outcomes compared to behaviors

We know for a fact that being able to produce the outcome "Client relationship that results in new business and revenue" is a requirement for success. Any successful person in a sales role would need to produce that outcome. But which behaviors in the list are important? It may be impossible to know for sure, and it might depend on whom you ask.

We are not saying that behaviors are not important, just that you should focus first on outcomes!

We are not saying that the behaviors are not important. After all, you can see how doing some of the behaviors well would help you produce the outcomes. But what we don't know is which behaviors are universal and would be done by any successful person. Which are more fruitful than others? In fact, at least one of the behaviors in Figure 12 depends on having a sales manager who is an ex-pro football player. Even if we wanted to perform the behavior, we could not. Most of us do not have an ex-pro football player as our manager!

Consequently, the WINNING Method focuses on the outcomes that a person must produce to be successful in a role. These are not arguable, and are not specific to an individual or his or her situation.

Why We Use Outcomes to Craft a Comprehensive Personal Plan for Breaking Tape

Outcomes are a key differentiator in the WINNING Method. Some books would simply ask you to list a bunch of goals and work those goals to achieve success. We ask you to identify the outcomes you will need to be able to produce to achieve your success. Identifying the outcomes associated with your success will enable you to create a more complete set of goals and to prioritize them. (You will do this in Step 6).

Let's say your wish is to earn a promotion in your company by year's end. You have selected a role model at your company who joined at about the same time as you and has already received two promotions. You ask them to identify the outcomes they produced that helped them achieve promotion. These might include:

- An internal champion (some senior manager) who recognized their capability, saw them as ready for a promotion, and could influence others.
- A professional-looking work portfolio that includes examples of work products and can be shared upwards to decision makers who create lists of candidates for promotion.

One key point is that outcomes are something you can *see* and *measure,* even if no one is present to observe their completion. Both of the outcomes above are tangible and measurable, not soft and squishy.

Here is another example: Let's say you were a forklift driver who loaded trucks every day. Your job was to get all the fresh produce in your firm's warehouse onto refrigerated trucks, and the trucks out on the road as quickly as possible, without damaging the produce. An outcome you would produce in this job might be: "all produce loaded, trucks underway, and loading dock empty by the end of my shift." That means that by the end of your shift, we should see no smashed produce on the dock, no produce bins waiting in the warehouse to go on trucks, and no trucks waiting to depart. This is something anyone can see and easily measure after you, the forklift driver, go home for the day.

Summary: Why Outcomes Matter

Let's wrap this up. Outcomes matter because when you know the outcomes you need to produce, you create a bridge to your wish and definition of success. Understanding the outcomes you will need to produce enables you to set the right goals to help you produce the outcomes. It also helps you identify the right strategies to close the gap between where you are today and where you want to be. This is why it is important to focus on outcomes first, before creating your goals. It is a critical step toward fast-tracking the construction of your personal plan for breaking tape.

Identifying Outcomes for Your Personal Plan for Breaking Tape

You can identify outcomes for your definition of success either by

- Observing them, as others around you produce them
- Or, interviewing a role model about them.

In either case, you will have good evidence that the outcomes will help you achieve the success you want. Let's look at each way we can identify outcomes for your personal plan for breaking tape.

Identifying Outcomes from Observation or Personal Knowledge

In some cases, you may immediately think of some critical outcomes you must be able to produce before you can achieve your success vision. This is true if...

- At work, you report directly to someone who is a role model for your success
- At home, you have chosen a role model with whom you already spend a great deal of time.

In both of these cases, you might be able to observe at least some of the outcomes they produce to achieve the success you desire.

Identifying Outcomes by Interviewing Your Role Model

Maybe you don't work closely with a role model. Or, you may be in a job that does not allow you to observe outcomes because they are produced by activity that is more mental than physical. Similarly, while you see your personal role model often, you are not confident that you have been able to observe all of the important outcomes they produce to achieve success. In these cases, we recommend you interview your role model again, this time to discuss his or her outcomes.

Warning—people don't normally talk to one another in terms of the "outcomes they produce" in their life or at work. You must ask the right questions to help them think in terms of outcomes versus behaviors.

People are used to talking to others about the things that they 'do,' but not necessarily about outcomes or results. They may perceive that results just happen, sometimes without great awareness.

Your job during this interview is to get your role model to talk about the outcomes they produce that enable them to achieve the success you desire. You want them to stay focused on the WHAT— the results and outcomes they produce, not the HOW. Chances are the WHAT (i.e., results) are something you will need to be able to produce to achieve your wish, even if the HOW (i.e., the behaviors and goals they used to get there) might be very different for you.

To help you with the task of gathering outcomes from your role model, we have provided some simple questions in the *Name the Outcomes that Matter Worksheet.* You can use this worksheet to keep your role model focused during the interview. Figure 13 is snapshot of the questions you can ask. The complete worksheet is included in the PDF worksheet packet on our website: http://breakingtape.com/worksheets.html.

With a little practice on your part, these questions will guide your role model to stay at a fairly high level. Using these questions with your role model will assist you in identifying and uncovering the outcomes that matter.

Name the Outcomes that Matter Worksheet
1. Enter your wish and definition of success: **Name and title (if needed) of your role model:**
2. Questions you can ask to help your role model formulate and articulate the outcomes he produced in support of his vision of success: • What did you produce, as a result of your efforts, which enabled you to achieve something similar to my wish or definition of success? • Optional: If many outcomes are provided, ask: Which of these were *most* important, or critical, in helping you succeed? • Did your mental mindset, or frame of thinking, help you to produce this outcome? If so, how? • What sorts of accomplishments or milestones did you have to meet to produce this outcome? • If you were to describe the big chunks of accomplishments that led to the successful production of the outcome, what would they be? NOTE: Use any or all of these questions to keep your role model focused on the outcomes he or she produced and note those outcomes in section 3.
3. Outcomes shared by your role model: (If more than three or four outcomes are provided, ask your role model to rank them.) Outcome: Notes: Outcome: Notes: Outcome: Notes:
4. Capture any roadblocks or success drivers your role model mentioned when discussing these outcomes: Roadblocks: Success Drivers:
Additional notes and comments made by role model:

Figure 13. Snapshot of key questions to keep the dialogue focused on outcomes

Selecting the Outcomes that Matter for Your Definition of Success

As you gather the outcomes that others have produced, you will quickly realize that not all outcomes are equal. Some will matter more than others. Some might be critical or of high importance. Others might have moderate or low impact on your definition of success. You want to select the three to four outcomes that are most critical, or have the most impact on achieving your wish and definition of success. So, if your role model shares seven to eight outcomes, ask him or her to rank them. After all, there is no need to focus on outcomes that will have little impact on your wish. Remember, knowing the right outcomes on which to focus will save you time and energy as you create your own personal plan for breaking tape.

In addition to rank ordering outcomes in terms of importance, think about how well these outcomes fit you. As you listen to the outcomes your role model shares, think about each of them in terms of your mental and physical capabilities, morals, and ethics. The important outcomes you focus on must be ones you can produce (perhaps with a new skill or two) and feel comfortable producing. Ask yourself, "Am I comfortable with the outcomes I am hearing from my role model? Are they morally and/or ethically in alignment with my work and life? Or, are they close enough to pursue without making me uncomfortable?"

During the interview and discussion with your role model about outcomes, an interesting thing may happen. As your role model begins to recall and feel more comfortable discussing outcomes, he or she may naturally think of and share related information. For example, many people will mentally chunk certain types of information together when they store it in memory. When they start talking about it (and pulling it out of memory), they may also tell you about related topics. As they tell you about an outcome, they may tell you some things that helped them (i.e., success drivers) or got in the way (i.e., roadblocks) as they tried to produce it. This is just the way our brains work.

If this happens, capture the possible roadblocks that can hinder you in achieving these outcomes. (Better to learn from others than discover these roadblocks for yourself!) Your role model may even suggest how to avoid them. Similarly, if they tell you things that helped them succeed, capture these success drivers for later use.

The worksheet you will use to capture outcomes has a space to jot down any roadblocks and success drivers you may hear during the interview. Just log them for now. In Step 4 we will show you how to use these roadblocks and drivers in the WINNING Method to unlock the power of your personal plan for breaking tape.

An Example

Here is an example to illustrate the process. Let's say you are an avid outdoor-type person who happens to like golf and plays the game pretty well. But you know your limitations, and you acknowledge that playing golf professionally is not a feasible success vision. However, you sure would like to be around a golf course and play whenever you can. Your wish is to find a way that golf can provide both enjoyment and profit in your life, without you having to become a professional golfer.

After much thought, you begin creating your personal plan by combining both a personal and worklife vision, following the first two steps in the WINNING Method:

1. You *wish, then define success* as: Owning and operating a profitable 18-hole golf course in the rolling hills of western North Carolina. (Nice vision!)

2. You have *identified and interviewed your role model:*

    • You find a small, family-run golf course in western North Carolina that has been in business (and making money) for over twelve years. Some key family members are willing to share with you their stories of how they did it.

    • They come from the same cultural thread as you. They are ethically and morally in alignment with your approach to business. Now you are ready to fast-track the creation of your personal plan by discovering their outcomes.

Next, meet with your role model again, this time to **name the outcomes that matter.** During the interview, your role model identifies six outcomes. In response to your request to rank order them, they tell you that the most important measurable outcomes they had to produce were:

  a. A geographical area where the average medium family income is over $50,000 and 50 percent of the population is over 50 years of age.
  b. Selection of a nine-hole golf course (with land available for nine more holes) that was designed by a respected professional golfer or golf course designer.
  c. Cash and/or investors' money on hand to carry the business for a minimum of four years from the purchase date.

As you think about these outcomes, you feel comfortable that the three most critical outcomes are good fits for you. While you realize that the third outcome (cash on hand) may take you time to produce, you have some savings and a good network to help you get started. None of the outcomes requires extensive new skills, and there are no moral/ethical issues. These are the three outcomes you choose to move forward with and transfer to your personal plan for breaking tape.

Closing Thoughts

This chapter guided you through the process of defining and naming the outcomes that matter. Outcomes are a key differentiator in both the WINNING Method and your personal plan for breaking tape. By spending the time to identify the outcomes associated with your success up front, you will be able to set and prioritize a more complete set of goals later. Focusing on outcomes also keeps you from being diverted by behaviors that look good but may not be productive for you.

If they are clearly observable, you can define the outcomes yourself. In most cases, you will need to interview a role model who will help you identify the most important outcomes. Gathering outcomes from your role model enables you to learn from others who have demonstrated the success you desire, which improves your chances of achieving it yourself.

If you capture and define them properly, outcomes will become important components of your personal plan for breaking tape, creating a practical, measurable bridge from your current situation to your wish and definition of success.

Keep your worksheets from this step handy for quick reference. You will use them for several of the WINNING Method steps that follow.

Motivational Checkpoint

1. Why do you think it is important to meet with a role model to identify the most important outcomes for your definition of success?

2. How is having a tight focus on results and outcomes going to help you make your definition of success a reality?

3. What kind of support would you like to have from your role model moving forward?

4. What are you excited about at this point in the process?

5. How well are you staying on track in the process? What do you need to do to keep yourself focused on your wish?

Work it Out

Apply the concepts and steps described in this chapter to complete this section of your personal plan for breaking tape.

Name the Outcomes that Matter

Directions:

1. Enter your wish or definition of success and the name and title of the role model in the spaces provided in Section 1 of this worksheet.

2. Ask the questions in Section 2 to uncover the most important outcomes this role model produces that support your success vision.

3. In Section 3, write and rank order the outcomes.

4. If any roadblocks or success drivers are shared, note them in Section 4.

Tip: Remember, listen carefully and note responses exactly as the role model states them. Don't be afraid to ask a question another way if you don't get the answer you need.

STEP 4

NOTE Success Drivers and Roadblocks

"Identify your roadblocks, but give complete focus and power to your success drivers and solutions." – Dennis Mankin

Don't you just hate to wait? We have a great success vision in mind. We've documented our wish and defined the outcomes that will help us achieve success. Why wait when we are ready to have it *NOW*!

But imagine for a moment that you have scheduled a trip to a wonderful place. Your anticipation is high—you are very excited about your destination. You can just see yourself there! In this situation, very few of us would just grab the car keys and head off on our trip. We've learned from other road trips that planning is essential to success. We have to pack the clothes and other things we anticipate that we will need. Our car may need gas or the maintenance we've been putting off. And we need to think about how we'll get there, who will drive, which roads we'll take, which ones we'll avoid, and where to stop along the way to get the most from our trip. Taking the time to plan pays off. We'll experience fewer problems and costs along the way, and we'll enjoy the journey more.

That's why this chapter on success drivers and roadblocks is so important to achieving your definition of success. The path you take to achieve your wish will have bumps in the road, or may even have a roadblock or two. For many people, there is a fine line between success and failure—it may come down to one bit of planning, or the avoidance of one big roadblock, pothole, or land mine. That's life. But achieving your success is TOO important to let it fall out of your grasp because of an unanticipated roadblock or failure to realize or use a personal success driver! Successful people learn how to anticipate and avoid the roadblocks that can halt progress and the land mines that can throw them off the road to success.

In Step 4, you will identify and anticipate the potential roadblocks, bumps in the road, and land mines that threaten your definition of success. You will also learn how to recognize the success drivers you can use to smooth out those bumps in the road and propel you safely past the roadblocks and land mines.

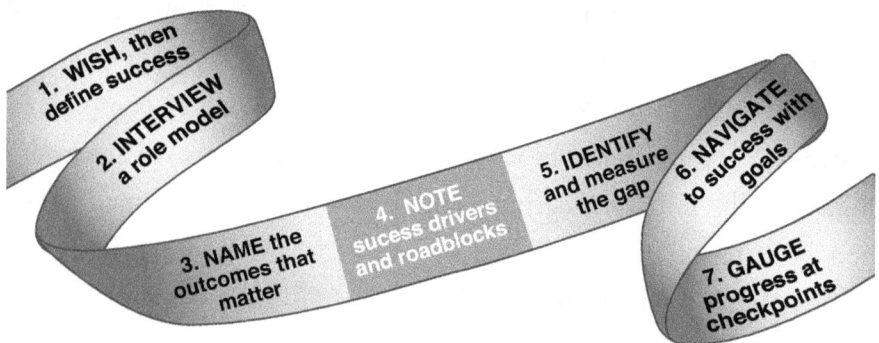

Figure 14. Ready for Step 4

In this chapter we will teach you

- What success drivers and roadblocks are
- How to identify and manage potential roadblocks on your path to success
- How to identify and leverage your personal success drivers to keep you moving along the path to success.

Why Focus on Success Drivers and Roadblocks?

Everyone knows capable, smart people who fail to achieve the success they want. Maybe it has happened to you. We have certainly experienced our own fair share of challenges. When this happens, people often blame one roadblock or land mine for throwing them off course and destroying their dreams. We've seen this over and over in our 30-plus years of work. Yet, we've also seen people who planned for and were able to avoid a similar roadblock altogether. *How? What made the difference?* A quote from T. Jay Taylor sums it up:

"Anticipate setback, anticipate defeat, and they will be but bumps on the road to long-term success." - T. Jay Taylor

Take the time to think about potential setbacks, what could defeat you, and how you will overcome these bumps on the road. Ask experts about how to accomplish an activity in their field, and they can tell you what to avoid and how to minimize errors and missteps. In fact, we are suggesting that you ask your role model to share roadblocks you should avoid, and discover how he or she leveraged personal strengths to do so. This is another reason we are such strong advocates of using role models. They have been down this road before, and they know where the bumps are. They also know what works, and you can use this information to make your trip smoother, saving you time and energy.

We've developed a four-box model that you will use later to assist you in anticipating and managing potential roadblocks by leveraging your personal success drivers. This is another key differentiator in our WINNING Method. By leveraging your success drivers to manage potential roadblocks, you can stay focused on the outcomes that matter.

The Importance of Being Positive—Even as You Consider Potential Roadblocks

We're going to ask you to think about potential roadblocks and land mines that could delay or derail your success. This is critical because it enables you to plan how you will avoid these roadblocks, if possible, and manage them, should they occur. As you think about these potential roadblocks, it is important that you stay *positive*. Yes, these roadblocks can derail your progress. And if you let them, they can take away your motivation. In other words, recognize potential roadblocks, but don't fear them.

> *"The only thing we have to fear is fear itself"- Franklin D. Roosevelt in his first inaugural address*

Our minds can play tricks on us. If you look out the side window while you are driving your car, you tend to move your car in that direction. If you keep reminding yourself not to slip on that last step, you may find yourself slipping on that step. Let your mind lead you to the fear, and the fear can become reality. Let your mind lead you to success drivers supporting your wish, and your wish can become your reality. As strange as it may seem, this is a fact.

We understand that it is easy to stumble and feel like not getting up, or to think about past failures and be tempted not to start. But knowing the enemy helps you prepare a strategy to fight it more effectively. And remember, you are not alone. The structure of our WINNING Method will guide you, even as you consider these potential roadblocks. After all, you will spend equal time thinking about the personal success drivers you can leverage to improve your journey.

Identifying Potential Roadblocks and Success Drivers

The four-box model in Figure 15 will help you identify both potential roadblocks and personal success drivers. The top two areas represent issues and circumstances that are external to you (outside of you)— your work environment, the physical resources you have available, etc.

The bottom two areas represent things that are internal to you (inside your body and mind)—your skills and personality traits, how you approach problems, and your motivation.

1. GENERAL ENVIRONMENT		2. RESOURCES AND SUPPORT
E X T E R N A L	• Is the environment in which you will be working to attain your wish conducive to your success? (e.g., a quiet space to think/work and record your progress, good lighting, etc.) • Are the general conditions for success (economics, social, family situation, manageable work commitments, etc.) in place? • Have you set aside adequate time to enable you to produce the outcomes that matter? • Can you devote the attention this effort requires, vs. being distracted by other big initiatives that might compete for your time and attention?	• Do you have the physical resources (e.g., money for necessary training, etc.) you will need to succeed? • Is your supervisor/manager (at work) or significant other (at home) supportive of your wish? • Do you have the big picture information you need to help you attain success? • Does your workplace, church, or other community group provide resources (e.g., tuition reimbursement, low-cost counseling, weight loss support, AA, or other health initiatives) to support your wish?
3. KNOWLEDGE, SKILLS, AND TRAITS		**4. APPROACH AND MOTIVATION**
I N T E R N A L	• Do you have all of the knowledge you will need to achieve your wish? • Do you have all of the skills you will need to achieve your wish? What are they? • Do you know which of your personal traits (e.g., procrastination, energy level, pessimism, etc.) could hinder your success? • Do you know which of your personal traits can help you achieve success?	• Is your success wish still clear to you, or does it need more definition? • Do you understand how you typically approach a new goal or vision, and has this worked for you in the past? • Do you know what motivates you, and how you stay motivated? • In the past, have you been able to sustain the level of motivation you have when you begin a new quest all the way through to its completion? • Are you aware of the roadblocks you fear most?

Figure 15. The Four-Box Model for Success Drivers and Roadblocks

In this model, roadblocks and success drivers represent opposites, as Figure 16 illustrates. Answering YES indicates the area of questioning is a success driver for you. Answering NO indicates a potential roadblock.

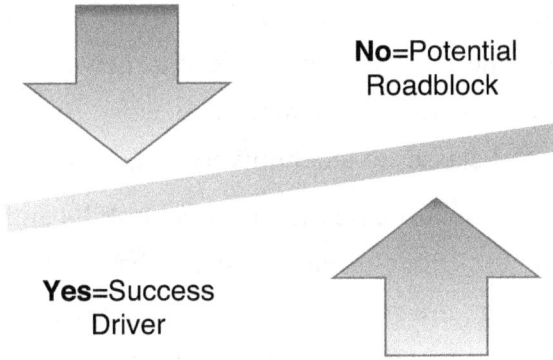

Figure 16. The Ying and Yang of Personal Roadblocks and Success Drivers

What are My Roadblocks and Success Drivers?

Set aside some quiet time. Work through each of the four boxes. Read the question, and then allow yourself to think both broadly and deeply about each area. Here are some tips to help you direct this thinking:

1. Recall past experiences that demonstrate the issue or area of questioning.

2. Visualize your current workplace and/or family environment.

3. Recall support other people have shown you, both at home and at work.

4. Think broadly about resources, beyond just physical resources such as money, a computer, or other tool to help you track your success, making sure you consider all of the resources available to help you achieve your wish.

5. Investigate support available to you that may not come to mind immediately. For example, many communities, churches, and other organizations provide free support ranging from resume design and job-hunting tips, to AA,

seminars, and workshops for parents and spouses, and advice and tools to help people start new businesses. Other community resources may also exist, such as low-cost informal classes at local universities.

6. Make an honest assessment of your skills and knowledge. What are your greatest strengths? What skills and knowledge are most relevant to achieving your wish and the outcomes you have defined? How can you use these skills and knowledge in new ways to help you manage roadblocks and achieve the success you desire?

7. Which personality traits might become roadblocks to you?

8. Which traits can become success drivers, helping to propel you to attain your vision?

9. How well has your approach to solving problems and attaining goals served you in the past?

10. How do you need to change your approach to achieve this success?

Use your answers to complete the *Personal Roadblocks and Success Drivers Worksheet* provided in the PDF worksheet packet. Figure 17 is a snapshot of the first section of this worksheet.

Personal Roadblocks and Success Drivers Worksheet		
Items Answered "Yes" (And Other Potential Success Drivers)	Items Answered "No" (And Other Potential Roadblocks)	My Plan to Leverage Success Drivers and Manage Roadblocks

ENVIRONMENT

Figure 17. Snapshot of a section of the Personal Roadblocks and Success Drivers Worksheet

Interviewing Your Role Model about Roadblocks and Success Drivers

Another valuable source of information about potential roadblocks and success drivers is your role model. In fact, he or she may have discussed things to avoid and tips for success during your last interview. If they did not, and you have access to your role model, ask to meet briefly again to discuss this topic. Role models have already been down this road and will have good ideas to share about potential roadblocks, success drivers they relied upon, and tips on their approach.

Here are some questions you can use to capture their ideas on potential roadblocks and how to avoid or manage them, and the skills, knowledge, traits, and approaches that helped them succeed. We also have organized these into the *Personal Roadblocks and Success Drivers Worksheet* that you can use when conducting the interview or documenting things they previously shared.

General Environment

1. How did your work and/or home environment contribute to your success?
2. Did you have to work around any special family situations, work commitments, or other special conditions to achieve success? If so, how did you do it?
3. How long did it take you, from start to finish, to achieve the success you wanted?

Resources and Support

4. Did you have the material resources (e.g., money and equipment) and support you needed to be successful? If so, what were they?
5. If you did not have the material resources and support you needed, what was missing and how did you work around it?

Knowledge, Skills and Traits

6. Did you have the knowledge and skills you needed to be successful, or did you have to acquire new knowledge or skill?
7. Which skills turned out to be most important to your success?
8. Which personality traits did you draw on to help you stay focused and on track as you set and worked toward your goals?

Approach and Motivation

9. How did you approach this achievement? For example, did you break it up into small bits, or stay focused on the big prize?
10. Did your approach change as you made this journey?

11. Which roadblocks did you face, and how did you manage them?

12. What kept you motivated even as you navigated the roadblocks?

After the interview with your role model is complete, find a quiet spot and review your notes from the session. Do you see any patterns and trends that reveal how your role model approached the journey, managed roadblocks, and leveraged his or her success drivers to keep going? Will any of these tips for approaching change work for you?

Closing

Compared to defining your success wish and outcomes, and choosing a role model, noting success drivers and roadblocks (Step 4) may seem trivial to you. But in fact, the insights you learn as you complete these activities will become an important key that will help you achieve your wish.

Few people take the time and effort to explore the success drivers that will enable their vision to become reality. This limits the possibility of success because we don't use the arsenal that is available to help us win! That's why in Step 4 of the WINNING Method we invite you to first look inward and reflect on the drivers you will need, and then outward, by asking your role model for tips from his or her experience.

Few people also take the time to identify potential roadblocks that can derail their success. The old saying, "What you don't know can't hurt you" is false. When we were children, we hesitated to look under the bed at night because some scary thing might be lurking there. As adults, we fear what we might discover if we start thinking about roadblocks to our success. But acknowledging potential roadblocks enables us to put strategies in place that will help us avoid them, and to manage and move past our fears. You don't drown by falling into water; you drown by staying there. So if you've experienced roadblocks before, acknowledge them, but find ways to move past them this time!

We cannot over-emphasize the importance of slowing down to do the important work in Step 4, so you can speed up to achieve your definition of success and ultimately your wish! If you take the time to do this essential step, not only are you more likely to finish the race, but also you will finish it with fewer bruises and less wasted energy.

Motivational Checkpoint

1. Which of your skills, knowledge, and traits will be most useful in smoothing the path and keeping you on track?
2. Which of the areas in the four-box model represent things that can sustain you as you work toward your vision?
3. To which of the areas in the four-box model do you plan to give most attention?

Work it Out

Apply the concepts and steps described in this chapter to complete this section of your personal plan for breaking tape.

Personal Roadblocks and Success Drivers

Directions. Answer the questions in the four-box model in Figure 15, using the *Personal Roadblocks and Success Drivers Worksheet* found in the PDF worksheet packet.

- If you answered "Yes," enter a summary of the item in the first column.
- If you answered "No," enter a summary of the item in the second column.
- Add other success drivers and roadblocks as they come to mind.

Then, summarize your plan in the third column of the *Personal Roadblocks and Success Drivers Worksheet*.

IDENTIFY and Measure the Gap

"You get what you measure." – Dr. Karen McGraw

If you have visited London, you have probably encountered the warning "mind the gap." It is all over the subway system, reminding travelers to take caution while stepping over the gap between the train door and the station platform. In some places the gap is big; in others it is small. Making the successful transition from the platform to the subway car (or vice versa) means paying attention to the size of the gap and adjusting your step accordingly. Minding the gap increases one's likelihood of success, while diminishing trips and falls.

Minding the gap makes sense in other parts of our lives, too. As you define the success you want, it pays to look at how big the gap is between your current reality and the reality you desire. If you underestimate the gap, you could trip yourself up by setting goals that won't get you all the way to your success. If you overestimate the gap, you might set bigger goals than you really need and end up being discouraged. An old adage says if you place the carrot too far out of reach of the rabbit, after a while, the rabbit will give up trying to get the carrot. And this same concept is true for us humans. Underestimate the gap in reaching your goal, or put it out of reach, and in time, you will give up trying.

This chapter on identifying (minding) and measuring the gap is very important to your success. You have defined the success you want and identified your role model(s). You've identified the outcomes that matter, as well as the success drivers and roadblocks that will help or hinder your journey. In this chapter you will use the WINNING Method to identify and measure the gap between where you are now in terms of the success you desire, and where you want to be at the end of this journey. Yes, it is a journey. The journey to your success could be a fast one or a journey with many goals to achieve on your way to success.

In Step 5, you will take an honest look at your current reality and identify the actual gaps that you will need to close on your way to success. You will put real measures on the gap(s) to establish where you are now, and what "done" looks like. Not only will this better prepare you to set the right goals at the right level (in Step 6), but it also will minimize trip-ups and missteps on your way to breaking your tape.

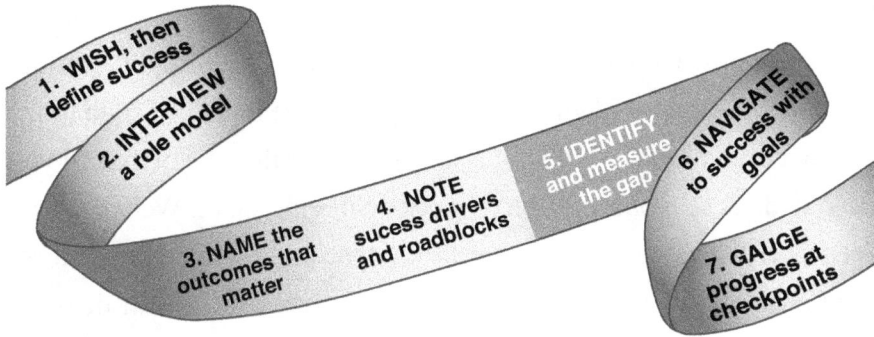

Figure 18. Ready for Step 5

In this chapter we will teach you:

- Why measuring gaps matters and will be a key differentiator in helping you succeed
- How to identify the personal or professional gaps that exist between your current reality and your desired reality
- How to measure the gap(s) between your current reality and future reality
- How to align these gaps and measures with the motivational factors that can help you close them.

Why Bother Measuring Gaps?

As the quote at the beginning of this chapter notes, "You get what you measure." Measuring something means that you are paying attention to it, focusing on it, and have the metrics to determine how you are doing. If you want change in your personal or professional life, you must measure the "before" to help you understand how to get to the "after."

Gaps First, Goals Later

You want positive change in your life or you would not be reading this book. You have identified what that change or future state looks like at a broad level. Many goal-based books will tell you that all you need to do is set goals and get to work achieving them. We have even seen goal "apps" on the market today that present a grocery-store-type checklist of goals you can choose to work on. Both of these approaches are wrong and frequently lead to discouragement or even abandonment of one's goals. You are not likely to be successful with a process that it is not geared specifically to you.

Identifying gaps before setting goals is one of the differences in the WINNING Method. Jumping into goal-setting without identifying and measuring the gap is like jumping into a lake without understanding how deep it is, how far you have to swim, and whether you feel that you can make it to the other side. If you've ever experienced this, you know that the result is often a lot of thrashing around, wasted energy—and in some cases, a return to where you started.

We want you to get to the other side and achieve the success you desire. We want you to be able to set goals that will get you there with the least effort and the fewest missteps. That is why this chapter focuses on identifying and then measuring gaps. You won't have to be conscious of these measures most of the time, but they are a very important part of your plan to break tape. Once your plan is set, these measures will help you commit to closing the gaps, defining better goals, and knowing when you have achieved your ultimate success.

Measurement and Rewards

Do you drive? Have you ever exceeded the speed limit? Probably yes. And, why did you exceed the speed limit? Because you can. If we don't get a ticket 99 percent of the time that we exceed the speed limit, most of us will speed a little sometimes. It is as simple as that. If some kind of electronic device in your car took $100 out of your bank account the moment you went over the speed limit, things might be different. Losing $100 may not be that punishing to you, but if it happened every time you exceeded the speed limit, you would probably change your behavior after a while.

If you want to change a behavior, you need to be able to measure it and reward your achievements in making the change. That's why we say "You get what you measure."

What we are talking about in our speeding example also applies to your identification and measurement of the gap between your current life or reality and what you want in your *future*. This is especially true of your wish, or definition of success. To increase your likelihood of success, we want you to define and put in measurable terms:

- Metrics that describe where you are today
- Measures that will indicate you have achieved the success you want
- The gap you must close to achieve your desired success.

Bottom Line—What Gets Measured Gets Done

People who achieve success both professionally and personally are usually the people who are honest with themselves about what they need to accomplish. They define and measure their success and are very mindful of and committed to their goals.

Here is what winners who are breaking tape do consistently:

- Identify and define, in measurable terms, where they are now and where they want to be in the future. Because they have these measures, they are able to determine clearly when they have closed their gap(s).
- Share their gap with others in their circle of friends and family to refine it and begin determining what must be done to close the gap. They ask others in their lives to hold them accountable and provide ongoing support and motivation.
- Write these measures next to their outcomes and put them where they can see them daily.
- Use their personal motivating factors to help them stay focused on what they need to do to close the gap and actualize their dream.

Sounds easy, right? The problem is that most people won't slow down long enough to identify the real gaps, establish metrics for where they are and where they want to be, and revisit their motivation to close the gap and achieve success. That would be a little like trying to set a destination in Google Maps without establishing your current location. The gap between where you are and where you want to be is what determines the route and helps estimate what it will take to reach the destination.

Defining and Measuring YOUR Gap

The sections that follow walk you through the steps for minding and measuring your gap(s).

1. Identify and define your gap

Let's start with the right mindset. You're identifying a gap because you want to get very specific in determining what you are going to have to do to close it. If it's a small gap, and you're almost there, you will be able to set fewer goals in Step 6 to close the gap. If it's a large gap, you may need to set intermediate goals or allow more time to close it. Intermediate goals are stepping stones that will be reasonable to achieve in a short time and reward you on your way to bigger goals. Regardless of the size of the gap, it's important to be very positive as you identify it. Don't let yourself be overwhelmed by the reality of the gap. Instead, realize that identifying the gap at this stage will improve your likelihood of success later. Knowing what we know, and also what we don't know, is powerful at this point in the WINNING Method. Not only do things that get measured get done, but by being very clear and honest with ourselves, they can be done well!

> *"What gets measured gets done: what gets measured and fed back gets done well; what gets rewarded gets repeated."*
> *- John E. Jones, leadership trainer*

Now, with this positive mindset, measure the gap between your current and future reality using metrics that make sense based on your situation. For example, let's say you want to be a manager at your firm. What measures could help define the gap? One of them is position level. How many positions are between your current job and a first-tier manager position? How many promotions will it take to get you to the manager position?

Another is level of responsibility. Managers have responsibility for directing the activity of some number of people. Do you currently have responsibility for other people, but in an informal way? If not, how many people must you manage to be formally considered a manager in your organization?

Some organizations also have a tenure requirement for managers. How many years of service are required at your firm to be able to hold a managerial position? How many years of service do you have currently?

Some organizations may also require that a manager have a college degree. If this is a requirement where you work, do you meet it? If not, does the firm waive the degree requirement based on years of experience in your industry?

As you see from this example, gap measures will vary based on the wish you have defined. In addition, you may need to do some research about the current situation you are trying to change to enable you to define your gap correctly and select the measures you should use.

Section 1 of the *Gap Worksheet* (Figure 19) included in the PDF worksheet packet provides spaces in which you can document your gaps at a high level.

Gap Worksheet			
1. Describe the gap between your current reality and your desired reality:			
Current reality	Current reality	Current reality	Current reality
Gap:	Gap:	Gap:	Gap:
Desired reality	Desired reality	Desired reality	Desired reality

Figure 19. Section 1 of the Gap Worksheet

2. Share your Gap to Refine it and Enlist Support

Defining your gap and initial measures is a great start. In this step you will refine it and enlist support from others. First, contact the role model you selected to help you make your wish a reality. Share the gap information you have captured so far and invite their insights on how they might close similar gaps. They may have a different perspective of the gap that will help you understand it better. Their experiences may have given them knowledge you don't have that could be useful in refining your gap.

If your role model does not have additional ideas, or cannot help you fill in missing information, ask if any of their contacts can help you get the information you need. Remember, the point here is to specify and understand completely the size of the gap.

You're going to need the help and support of others beyond your role model to make the changes required to attain your wish. Enlist the support of significant others, friends, your manager, or peers as you define the gap and measures. Remember, "Knowledge is power."

3. Link these Measures to the Outcomes you Defined Previously (and the Goals you Define Later)

In Step 3 of the WINNING Method, you identified the outcomes that you would need to be able to produce in order to attain your wish. This is a good time to look back at the outcomes you defined, this time from the perspective of closing the gap:

- Examine each measure you identified to close the gap. Can you align it with at least one outcome?
- If you can, document the outcomes associated with the measures on Section 2 of the *Gap Worksheet* included in the PDF worksheet packet.
- If not, consider whether you need to update your outcomes or refine your measures.

Specific measures (the data you will seek and use to monitor your progress) will help you keep it real and give you tools to track your progress.

"In God we trust; all others must bring data."
- W. Edwards Deming, statistician, professor, author

Before you read further, take the time to complete the first three columns in Section 2 of the *Gap Worksheet*, aligning each gap with an outcome, refining your gaps, and documenting the measures you identified to close each gap.

4. Use your Personal Motivating Factors to Drive you Toward your Success and Close the Gap

In the previous chapter you identified your own success drivers that will help propel you toward the finish line and the wish you desire. Revisit those success drivers now, reflecting on them as you ask these questions:

- Which of these motivating factors are the most powerful in helping me close the gap?
- Are there other motivating factors that I can activate and apply as I work to close the gap?

Write your answers to these questions in the final column in Section 2 of the *Gap Worksheet*.

The importance of motivation and emotional maturity in closing gaps between where you are today and where you want to be cannot be overstated. One of the most important keys to closing your gap successfully is to understand that you have the power to change your expectations for yourself and the value you place on attaining your wish. Being emotionally mature means living with integrity, being present, and embracing the reality of who you are. Being emotionally mature also means being responsible for the choices you make in life and having a clear vision of what you want personally and professionally; your wishes for success.

Take a moment now to complete Section 3 of the *Gap Worksheet,* reflecting on your gaps.

Closing Thoughts

This chapter guided you through the process of identifying, refining, and measuring the gap(s) between your current reality and your desired reality. By identifying gaps before you set goals, you increase your likelihood of success. You shared your gaps with your role model and enlisted the support of others to make changes required to close gaps and attain your wish.

Finally, you revisited your personal motivating factors, including the emotional maturity factors and success drivers to understand how you can apply them as you work to close your gaps. This important motivational component contributes to success and can make the difference between eventual success or failure.

Motivational Checkpoint

1. Which of the measures to close the gap will be the easiest to attain?

2. Which of the measures to close the gap will require the most effort on your part?

3. List at least three reasons it is important for you to close the gap.

Work it Out

Apply the concepts and steps described in this chapter to complete this section of your personal plan for breaking tape.

My Gap Worksheet

Directions: Document the gaps that exist between your current and future realities in Section 1.

In Section 2, align gaps with outcomes and document measures and motivations for each gap.

In Section 3, reflect on your gaps and measures.

STEP 6

NAVIGATE to Success with Goals

"Even if you're on the right track, you'll get run over if you just sit there." – Will Rodgers, American humorist and actor

You are on your way to success! You know you are on the right track if you've completed five of the steps in the WINNING Method. But Will Rodgers was right; don't stop now! It's time to set the goals that will propel you toward the finish line and enable you to make your wish a reality.

You're probably thinking, "Here we go again with how to set goals. I've heard it a hundred times!" You may be surprised to hear that we tend to agree with you! Like you, we've read countless books, blogs, and articles on topics such as setting goals, the importance of having goals in our lives, how to achieve goals, and so on. We have seen apps for setting and tracking goals. And, we've listened to motivational speakers emphasize the virtues of setting and achieving goals. We get it—and concur—goals are important!

With so much information about goals available, why is it that many of us have failed miserably in accomplishing the goals we set? And what makes the WINNING Method any different from the other approaches to setting and achieving goals?

Like many of you, we learn through experience, trial, and error. Over the course of 30 years, we've used many goal-setting methods in our own work and personal lives, and sometimes we've even achieved success with them. We've also discovered some important factors that made the difference between goal success and failure— both for us, and the people with whom we've worked. We've learned what works, as well as what doesn't. We understand the roles that personal motivation, commitment, and being grounded play in goal achievement. And we've used these lessons learned to create a new, improved, goal-setting strategy. Finally, we've applied our goal-setting strategy in the worlds of business, human performance improvement (HPI), and coaching.

The purpose of this chapter is to share these valuable lessons and our goal-setting strategy with you. We want you to think about goals as waypoints that will guide you toward your destination—success! Like a good sailor, you already know where you want to go—your destination is attaining the wish you defined when you started this book. The outcomes you have already identified set the course and specify what you must be able to produce to attain your wish. But it is the goals you set that will enable you to navigate consistently across your gap, toward success.

In Step 6 of the WINNING Method you will set goals to close the gap between your current reality and your wish. You will create at least one goal that will help you attain each outcome. You will determine how you can activate the success drivers you identified in Step 4 to propel you toward the finish line. You will check to make sure that the goals you set will close the gap you identified in Step 5. Finally, you will refine your goals, getting feedback from your role model. We will walk you through this step-by-step and share examples along the way.

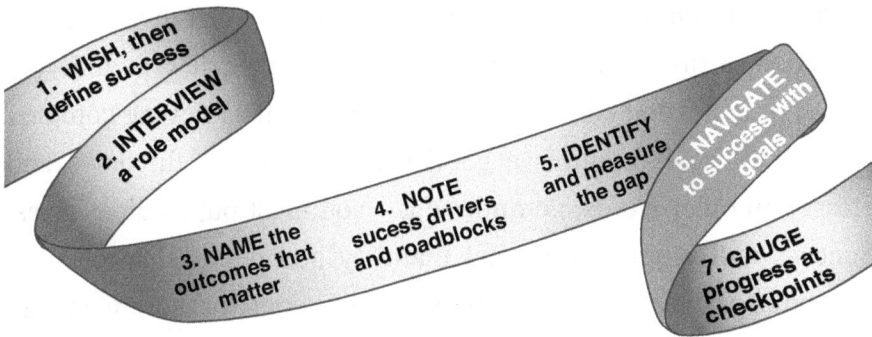

Figure 20. Ready for Step 6

In this chapter we will teach you:

- Why people fail to meet goals
- What our BREAK-through Goal Strategy is, and why it works where others have failed
- How to use the BREAK-through Goal Strategy to craft great goals that set the stage for your success.

Goal Basics

Before we discuss how to set better goals, let's take a look at some important goal basics.

Definition

First, let's agree on what a goal is. Our definition of a goal is (Figure 21): *an action with a desired result, a measure of success, and a timeframe, in which a person believes and can commit to achieving.*

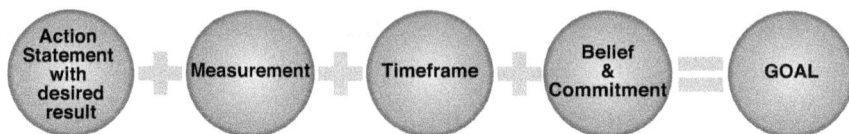

Figure 21. Goal definition

Many definitions of goals exist, and most specify that there must be an action, a timeframe, and a measure. However, few include the notion of belief and commitment. We know that achieving complex or difficult goals requires a good focus, long-term diligence and effort—in other words, commitment. You must put aside excuses. Success will require emotional maturity and personal motivation on your part. Your action statement, plus your measurement and timeframe for your goals, along with the belief that you can achieve them, will greatly affect your success.

Goals are Tools

Goals are powerful tools that help you think about how you will make your wish a reality. If you define them right, your goals will motivate and enable you to produce each outcome your success requires. All successful people use some type of goal setting. Whether you are a business leader, a musician, a middle manager, a florist, a consultant, or an athlete, you probably have set goals to help focus yourself on success.

Let's say you're a runner and that your wish is to run a 10K marathon. If you have just started running, this is a very big wish. If the gap between how far you can run today and the wish you have set is too great, you will hit the wall during your first race when that feeling of fatigue and hopelessness overwhelms you.

No one goal will get you from running around the block to running a 10K. You will need a mix of goals to build up your ability to complete the 10K. Some goals may focus on your physical preparation and nutrition, others on your mental preparation. Some might have a short-term deadline or timeframe, while others may have a more distant deadline.

You already have a good foundation for the 10K—you have used the WINNING Method to begin creating your personal plan to break tape. You have defined a wish, and have worked with a runner role model to identify the outcomes you need to produce to enable you to complete the 10K. You know your success drivers and roadblocks. You have examined the gap between how far you can run today and the run you'd like to complete. Now it's time to set very specific goals that you can use as tools to build your capability and strength and to keep you motivated.

Why People Fail to Meet Goals, and What to Do About It

Before you set the goals that will drive you toward success, let's examine why so much is written about goals: *It is simply because most people fail to meet the goals they set.* Understanding *why* people fail to meet goals will help you avoid common mistakes and improve your chances of success.

People fail to meet goals either because of problems related to how they set the goals, or to personal factors that affect their goals. In Table 1, we present a list of the most common reasons people fail to meet goals, along with tips to eliminate or lessen the impact of each potential problem.

Table 1. Tips for Lessening the Impact of Common Goal Problems

Reasons People Fail to Meet Goals	Tips
Goals are talked about and verbalized but never written down.	Write them down! If you don't commit them to writing, they don't seem real.
Goals are vague and general.	People typically don't achieve general goals. They meet personal goals that matter to them. Craft your goal statement so that it matters to you.
Goals lack either measures or a definite timeframe. Without these two components, how do you know when you have reached the goal?	Make sure every goal you create has a definite timeframe and some way to measure your progress and completion.
Goals are not tied to specific outcomes or are not aligned with your motivation. They are fuzzy goals that aren't grounded in anything important.	Ground your goals. Align and lash them tightly to the outcomes that will get you to your wish. Every goal should have a purpose and help you achieve something important.
Goals are sized improperly. They are so big and ambitious that you fear failure, or too small to make you care about achieving them.	Take the Goldilocks approach—your goals should be "just right," not too big or too small.
You set too many goals, which makes it impossible to focus on any one of them	You know yourself better than anyone. How many goals can you, personally, attend to at any one time? If it's not many, then prioritize them and start working on the top one or two first.
You don't believe that you can achieve the goal or you lack the emotional maturity to follow through with your goals.	Recognize that your negativity may be irrational. Write down the goal, and then write three reasons (your skill, your personality, your experience, etc.) why you know you can meet it. If you start feeling negative, go back and read the goal and the reasons again.
You lack support to help you refine your goal or to nudge you along toward completion.	Seek help from the role model you selected for your wish, or from another trusted person at home or at work. He or she probably would be more than willing to help you refine your goals.
You fail to monitor your progress at regular checkpoints or take responsibility for success.	Our next chapter provides you with a process you can use to set logical checkpoints and gauge your progress as you are working toward goal completion. Take responsibility for your forward progress. Own it and work your goal to achieve the success you desire.
You start strong but lose focus because your motivation is in the moment, not in the goal or its achievement.	At each goal checkpoint, take a moment to congratulate yourself on the progress you have made and to think about all the positive things that will be associated with completing the goal. Find ways to keep your motivation and commitment high throughout the process.
Not achieving a goal becomes a terminal event. You give up, rather than refining and revising the goal and trying again.	Remember, meeting goals requires emotional maturity. If you are emotionally mature, you will move on after setbacks, confident in your ability to succeed eventually. Instead of giving up when you become frustrated, analyze problems, seek solutions, and choose the best path to get you back on track.

Have you experienced any of these common reasons we don't achieve our goals? If so, don't give up. All of us have experienced one or more of these in the past and we may face them again. Tap into your emotional maturity to try again, but this time, try something new—our *BREAK-through Goal Strategy.*

The BREAK-through Goal Strategy— What It Is and Why It Works

This is not a book about goals; it is about an approach to winning at work and life. However, the goals you set are essential to your personal plan for breaking tape. Our *BREAK-through Goal Strategy* is a part of the WINNING Method. It is a tool—a powerful one—to help you set and manage goals as you work to attain your success.

We named it the *BREAK-through Goal Strategy* because it will help you break through obstacles and attain goals on your way to success. We use the word 'BREAK' as a powerful yet simple way to remember how to create goals you can put into action to move you toward your personal finish line. Each letter in 'BREAK' represents an important concept or factor based on research and best practice in goal setting:

- **B**-Believable—the goal is something you can believe in
- **R**-Realistic—the goal is feasible and achievable
- **E**-Explicit—the goal uses specific, action-oriented language—do what, by when
- **A**-Activate—the goal activates your personal motivation system, engaging and challenging you in such a way that you want to do it

- **K**-Key measure(s)—the goal statement contains measures that will enable you to know when you have met the goal

The *BREAK-through Goal Strategy* works because it is based on tested research and best practices for goal-setting success:

- The *BREAK-through Goal Strategy* is systematic. You don't just pull goals from the air or choose them from a list. You don't even consider setting goals until you understand how big the gap is between where you are today and where you need to be to attain your wish. Instead of being the first step in the process, goal setting is the sixth step in the WINNING Method. The work you have done before this step will give you the grounding and personal understanding you need to set the right goals, at the right level.

- The *BREAK-through Goal Strategy* aligns the goals you set directly to the outcomes you must achieve. This means you won't be tempted to list a bunch of activities you think you need to do. Instead, you will be defining the actions you need to take to produce each outcome you have defined. Here's a boating analogy to illustrate. You could just get in a sailboat, raise the sails, and head out to sea (a set of activities), determining where you want to go based on the direction of the wind. But this won't get you to your desired port within a specific time, especially if it is a long distance from where you are starting. Instead, your outcomes become the ports on the way to your final destination— your wish. The goal(s) you set to reach each port become waypoints, or references, that help you get to the port.

- The *BREAK-through Goal Strategy* helps you craft your goals in a way that draws you in, activating your belief system and personal motivation. Researchers[1] have identified principles of successful goal setting. They determined that to motivate us to meet a goal, it must be: *clear* (measurable, specific), *challenge* us (draw us in, motivate us to succeed), and *enable* us to commit to it (e.g., is something we think we can do).

We built these best practices into our *BREAK-through Goal Strategy*. The first best practice is reflected in three factors of our strategy: the goal is realistic (R), explicit (E), and includes key measures of success (K). To address the second best practice, we established the factor "activates your personal motivation system" (A) so that you *want* to do it. To address the third best practice, we established the factor "believe it is something you can do" (B).

Our *BREAK-through Goal Strategy* won't achieve results by itself, however. You will have to invest personally in both goal setting and goal completion. As we've noted before, success requires emotional maturity and personal motivation. *The depth of your belief in your ability to meet your goal will affect its achievement.* Our strategy forces you to think about a goal's believability, its ability to challenge and motivate you, and your commitment to it as you set and refine it. In the end, *you* are responsible for making it a reality.

---

1   Locke, E. and Latham, G.P. (2006). "New Directions in Goal-Setting Theory," Volume 15—Number 5, Association for Psychological Science.

Locke, E.A., & Latham, G.P. (1990). A Theory of Goal Setting and Task Performance. Englewood Cliffs, NJ: Prentice-Hall.

"A vision without a plan is just a dream.
A plan without a vision is just drudgery.
But a vision with a plan can change the
world." – Old Proverb

How to Use the BREAK-through Goal Strategy to Create Your Goals

Ready to start creating great goals that will help you attain your wish? In this section we take you, step by step, through the *BREAK-through Goal Strategy* (Figure 22). All you need are a few 3x5 index cards, and a pencil or pen.

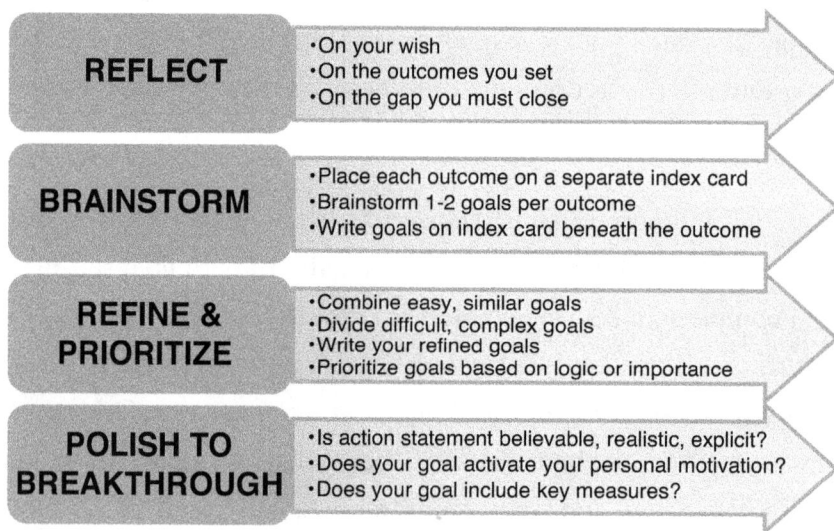

REFLECT	•On your wish •On the outcomes you set •On the gap you must close
BRAINSTORM	•Place each outcome on a separate index card •Brainstorm 1-2 goals per outcome •Write goals on index card beneath the outcome
REFINE & PRIORITIZE	•Combine easy, similar goals •Divide difficult, complex goals •Write your refined goals •Prioritize goals based on logic or importance
POLISH TO BREAKTHROUGH	•Is action statement believable, realistic, explicit? •Does your goal activate your personal motivation? •Does your goal include key measures?

Figure 22. BREAK-through Goal Strategy

Let's walk through the four primary steps of our *BREAK-through Goal Strategy.* In each step there are some simple yet very important questions and statements you need to reflect on to set and refine your goals to ensure your success.

1. REFLECT. The first step in the *BREAK-through Goal Strategy* is the basis upon which you will develop your goals. You will use your personal plan for breaking tape to complete this step. Table 2 illustrates.

Table 2. Guide for Reflection

Reflect, then act on these statements	Actions	Note any thoughts or comments to remember about this statement
Revisit and think about your Wish	Recall your vision of success and what it means to attain your Wish	
Recall any discussions you had with your role model about what it will take to achieve these outcomes	Make note of the activities your role model shared with you	
Remind yourself why it is important for you to attain these outcomes	Think of the positive changes this will mean to you	
Review the outcomes you defined in Step 3 and visualize yourself being able to produce each of the outcomes	Visualize yourself finishing each of the outcomes and taking the positive steps toward your Wish	
Think about what you will have to do to prepare yourself to produce each outcome	Note what you will do to prepare yourself to produce each of these outcomes	
Think realistically about the gap you identified in Step 5. Don't overestimate or underestimate the gap	Confirm that the outcomes you defined will help you close this gap. This is the basis upon which you will develop your goals	

2. BRAINSTORM. This step relies on a creativity technique to assist you in stimulating goal ideas for each of your outcomes. Let ideas for goals that tie back to achieving your specific outcomes spontaneously come to mind.

Start by putting each of the outcomes you defined on a separate index card. (See example in Figure 23.)

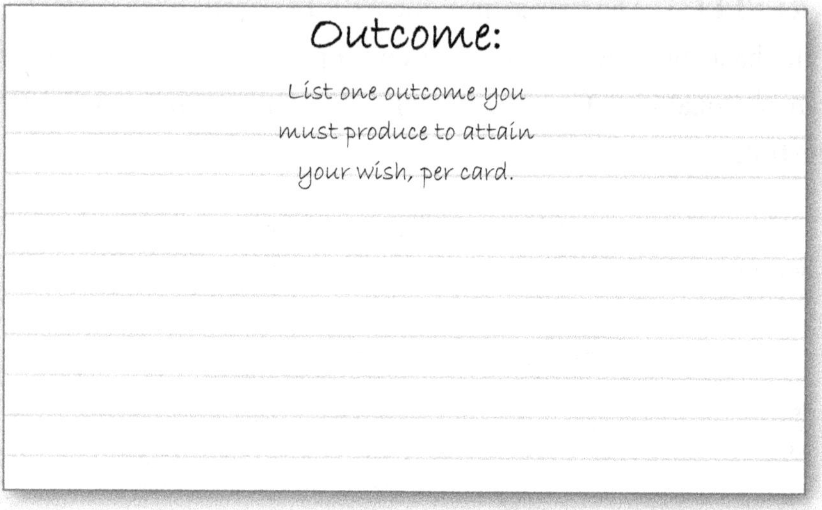

Outcome:

List one outcome you
must produce to attain
your wish, per card.

Figure 23. Sample 3"X 5" index card; list one outcome per card

Pick up the first outcome/index card and think about what you must be able to do to produce it. Brainstorm possible goals you could set, that when met, would enable you to produce the outcome. Don't limit yourself to what has worked or not worked in the past. Brainstorming is looking at what *could* be possible. Use the following goal structure to draft your goals:

- **Action statement**: What you will do. Be very clear and specific about exactly what you will do. No fuzzy statements allowed.
- **Measurement**: Your target measures that, when met, will signal achievement.
- **Timeframe**: The time within which you will meet your goal.

Write the draft goals beneath the outcome. Use the same process to construct one to two goals for each outcome.

Let's look at an example in which your wish is to become a professional project manager. One of the main outcomes to help you attain this wish is "Projects delivered on time and within budget." If you are brainstorming goals for this outcome, you might come up with draft goals such as the following:

- Complete all required work for the "Introduction to Project Management" course within the next two months
- Create a work breakdown structure (WBS) for an actual project within the next quarter that is accepted by the Project Manager
- Successfully manage a small, two- to three-person project within the next 10 months.

Figure 24 illustrates putting these draft goals on a 3"X 5" outcome card.

> ## Outcome:
> Projects delivered on time and within budget.
>
> ## Goals leading to Outcome:
> 1. Complete all required coursework for the "Introduction to Project Management" course within the next two months
>
> 2. Create a work breakdown structure (WBS) for an actual project within the next quarter that is accepted by the Project Manager
>
> 3. Successfully manage a small, two-to-three-person project within the next 10 months

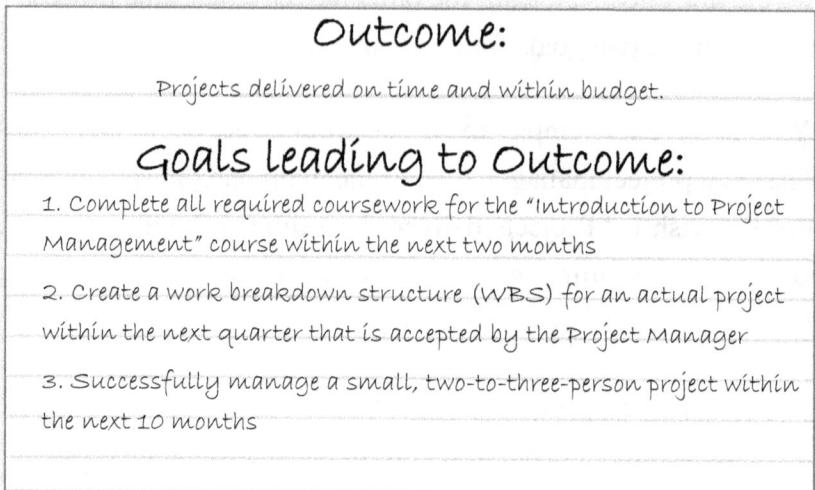

Figure 24. Example of Outcome and Goals on 3"X 5" card

Don't get sidelined by whether your goals are perfect yet. You are using brainstorming guidelines to capture your ideas for possible goals in this step. Be open to what is possible! Right now, it is good enough to get some goals you can work with on your index cards. You will refine, prioritize, and polish them later.

3. REFINE AND PRIORITIZE. Before you move ahead with these goals, you want to do two important things: Refine them (if needed) and prioritize them. This step in the *BREAK-through Goal Strategy* helps you create goals with a clear focus and great impact on your outcomes. Take the draft goals you brainstormed for each outcome and look at each goal individually. Ask yourself the questions in Table 3 to begin refining your draft goals.

Table 3. Questions and Options to Refine and Prioritize Goals

Questions to ask yourself	Options to take
Can you reword any goal to make it more clear or explicit?	If **yes:** Reword the goal
	If **no:** Keep the goal as is
Do any of the goals for one outcome sound similar or accomplish the same thing?	If **yes:** Combine them into a single goal statement without making it too complex
	If no: Keep the goal as is
Do any of your goals: • Sound difficult, outrageous, or complex? • Take more than one measure to determine if you met it? • Make it difficult to manage your progress and succeed as written?	If **yes:** Break the goal into two or more goal statements
	If **no:** Keep the goal as is

For example, one of the draft goals from the previous step was: "Successfully manage a small, two-to three-person project within the next 10 months." You can reword this to make it more explicit, as shown in Table 4.

Table 4. Refining an Original Goal

Original Goal	Challenge with Goal as Written	Refined Goal
Successfully manage a small, two-to three-person project within the next 10 months.	1. The word **"successfully"** is ambiguous. You could be more explicit by saying **"on time and in budget"** 2. The word **"small"** is really not necessary since you describe the number of people as two to three. You could eliminate it.	Manage a two- to three-person project to completion, on time and in budget, within the next 10 months.

Finally, it might be difficult to work on all the goals for an outcome at the same time without losing momentum or sacrificing a goal by juggling too many. Can you prioritize your goals so that you can work on one or two things at a time?

To prioritize, think about the wish you are trying to achieve and the outcome the goal supports. Ask yourself:

- Is there a logical order in which you should complete your goals?
    - o   If no logical order exists, can you prioritize your goals based on the ones that are most important to complete first?
    - o   Which ones are *most* critical to your ability to produce the outcome?
- Another way to prioritize your goals is to think about your personality.
    - o   Are you the kind of person who likes to do the easy goals first to build confidence and momentum, or
    - o   Do you prefer getting the hard tasks or goals out of the way first?

In our project management example, the order in which goals were originally captured already represents a logical order that you could use to prioritize what you do first. After you have prioritized the goals for each outcome, ask yourself, "If I met all of these goals, would I achieve all of the outcomes?" At this point your answer should be "Yes." If not, you need to look for goals that may be missing and add them to your list.

If I met all of these goals, would I achieve all of the outcomes?

Write your refined and prioritized goals in the second column of the *BREAK-through Goals Worksheet* shown as Figure 25 and included in the PDF worksheet packet.

BREAK-through Goals Worksheet		
Outcome	**Refined Goals, Prioritized** Reword, combine similar goals, and break complex goals into multiple goals	**Polished Goals** (Believable, Realistic, Explicit, Activates personal motivation, includes Key measures)
Outcome 1:	Goal 1: Goal 2: Goal 3:	Goal 1: Goal 2: Goal 3:
Outcome 2:	Goal 1: Goal 2: Goal 3:	Goal 1: Goal 2: Goal 3:
Outcome 3:	Goal 1: Goal 2: Goal 3:	Goal 1: Goal 2: Goal 3:
Outcome 4:	Goal 1: Goal 2: Goal 3:	Goal 1: Goal 2: Goal 3:

Figure 25. Snapshot of the BREAK-through Goals Worksheet

4. POLISH TO BREAKTHROUGH. In this final step you will polish your goals and be sure that they are in a finished state that will work for your purposes.

Use the third column of the *BREAK-through Goals Worksheet* to polish your refined, prioritized goals. First, review each refined goal against the BREAK-through factors: Believable, Realistic, Explicit, Activates personal motivation, and Key measures. Then polish each goal as needed to create great, workable goals that you are motivated to achieve. In many cases you may not have to add much to your goal to motivate you to complete it. In others, you may need to tweak the wording to activate your personal motivation and commitment.

For example, let's say that you don't particularly enjoy being in a classroom, yet you must take the Introduction to Project Management course to become a professional project manager. The draft goal was: "Complete all required coursework for the Introduction to Project Management course within the next two months."

To motivate yourself and commit to this goal (when you don't like being in a classroom), you might need to polish it to something like: "Achieving a certificate for completing the Introduction to Project Management course by attending virtual and/or classroom sessions within the next two months."

The focus now becomes the certificate—a *reward* for completing something you don't really like—a reward that will position you for future success! And to address your dislike of classroom training, you have indicated that you can complete the course with a mix of virtual and classroom sessions. The goal is set and you are another step closer to your wish!

"A goal properly set is halfway achieved."
– Zig Ziglar, motivational speaker and author

Your goal setting work is now complete! Use the *BREAK-through Goals Checklist* (Figure 26) in the PDF worksheet packet to make sure you have set great goals that will guide you to success.

X	#	Checklist Item
	1.	Do you have at least one goal for each outcome defined?
	2.	Does *each* goal conform to the suggested goal structure? ACTION STATEMENT | MEASUREMENT | TIMEFRAME
	3.	Is each goal something you can **believe** in, and get behind?
	4.	Is each goal **realistic** and achievable?
	5.	Is each goal **explicit** and clearly stated so you know exactly what you must do to meet it?
	6.	Does each goal, as stated, **activate** your personal motivation so that you want to achieve it?
	7.	Is there at least one **key measure** for each goal so that you will know when the goal has been met?
	8.	Is each goal just big enough to be motivating without being too challenging and complex?
	9.	Have you combined goals that are very similar in content?
	10.	Have you prioritized the goals for each outcome?

Figure 26. Snapshot of the BREAK-through Goals Checklist

Closing Thoughts

This chapter guided you through the process of setting great goals that are:

- Believable
- Realistic
- Explicit
- Activate your personal motivation
- Key measures

We have discussed why people fail to meet goals and taught you how to use the *BREAK-through Goal Strategy* to greatly improve your success. We have shared with you the importance of personal belief and motivation in goal achievement. Motivation is not something you will turn on and off during your journey to achieve success. In this chapter, you have activated your personal motivation as you set goals you can believe in and can commit to. But you will have to *stay* motivated and build on that motivation as you work the goals you set today.

You have accomplished a lot and have workable goals to show for it! Now it is time to begin *working* on the goals you have set. Commit today to begin your journey to meet each goal! Remember, this is not a book about goals; it is about an approach to winning at work and life that can change your life for the better.

Motivational Checkpoint

1. Which of the goals you set will be the easiest to attain?

2. Which of the goals you have set will require the most effort?

3. List the two goals about which you are most passionate and motivated.

4. Do you feel that any goals could be a struggle to achieve or a potential problem? If so, use a table like the one that follows to build your confidence and positivity.

Goals that Could Be a Struggle to Achieve, or a Potential Problem	Three Reasons (skill, personality, experience, motivation, etc.) Why I Know I Can Meet the Goal
Goal:	1. 2. 3.
Goal:	1. 2. 3.
Goal:	1. 2. 3.

Work it Out

Apply the concepts and steps described in this chapter to complete this section of your personal plan for breaking tape.

BREAK-through Goals Worksheet

Directions. Document your refined goals for each outcome and prioritize them. Then take a hard look at each goal, polishing each one to make sure it follows the BREAK-through model.

BREAK-through Goals Checklist

Directions. Use this checklist to make sure you have developed great goals that will lead you to 'breaking tape' and help you achieve your wish. Place an "X" beside each item to confirm that your goals comply.

STEP 7

GAUGE Progress at Checkpoints

"Those who do not move, do not notice their chains."– Rosa Luxemburg, economist and philosopher

You know what you want to accomplish; you've set your goals. Now it's time to work them. It's tempting to think that Nike was right — "Just do it."[1] Sounds simple, right? After all, isn't making progress toward our wish just a matter of achieving all of our goals?

Sure, if you're exceptionally focused and extremely experienced in this business of setting and achieving goals. Most of us are not. It's possible to set your sights on a goal and measure your progress by whether or not you attain it. But for many of us, success will come step by step. That's why it's important to look at your goals and set reasonable checkpoints along the way to help you achieve them. These checkpoints allow you to take one bite at a time as you work toward your goal.

---

1   Just do it is a trademark of Nike.

---

*"When eating an elephant, take one
bite at a time."- Creighton Abrams, Jr.,
American military leader*

Checkpoints make it easier to stay motivated because you can see your own progress and not be overwhelmed by the size of your goal. They also allow you to gauge your progress at regular intervals and monitor the behaviors that will lead you to goal success. If you don't gauge your progress and keep track of your progress it's easy for goals to slip away. You know the old expression: "out of sight, out of mind"? If you're monitoring your progress on a regular basis, your goal stays 'in sight' and 'in mind.'

In Step 7 we will teach you some simple techniques to define, set, and use checkpoints to monitor, gauge, and log your progress. We encourage you to celebrate your progress as you achieve each milestone, and create long-term, positive habits for life.

Using Step 7 of the WINNING Method, you will create the final piece of your personal plan for breaking tape and celebrate your successes as you achieve them!

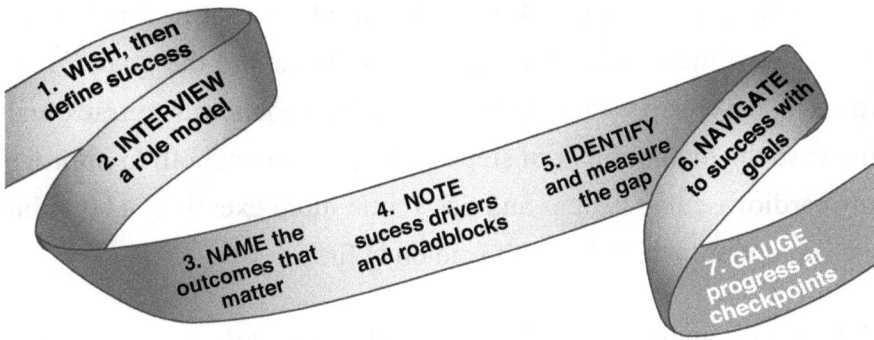

Figure 27. Ready for Step 7

In this chapter we will teach you:

- Techniques for defining and setting checkpoints to accomplish complex or difficult goals
- How to use checkpoints to monitor, gauge, and log your progress
- The importance of celebrating your improvements at checkpoints on your way to achieving your goals and wish.

A Personal Example

Let's start with a personal example from Dennis.

As a part of my 'get healthy' wish this year, I set a goal to increase the number of steps I took each day by 50 percent, improve my cardiovascular capacity, and burn more calories each day. To help me gauge my progress, I have been wearing a Fitbit (www.fitbit.com), a device that enables me to track the number of steps I walk each day, the total miles I walk, and the estimated calories I burn.

Now, I wasn't a total wreck when I started my 'get healthy' wish, and I knew the outcomes I needed to achieve and the goals I had to set to make my wish a reality. One of my goals was to track and increase the total number of steps I take each week, both to improve my cardiovascular system and get a little more exercise. The Fitbit was an option, which I wasn't sold on at first.

A Fitbit is a small electronic device that you hook on your pocket or belt to monitor simple motions of your body. Within a few days, I was hooked. I found it very helpful to monitor my progress each day against the goal I had set. The Fitbit synchs up with my computer or phone whenever I am near them. In other words, it automatically gauges my progress. I'll admit, sometimes the information can be a bit too much! But since I have daily checkpoints, it makes monitoring my progress simple. Being able to see my progress against daily checkpoints has had a huge impact on helping me achieve my goal. (This is not a promo for Fitbit, but it is a promo for the importance of gauging progress against checkpoints at regular intervals.)

For example, I started with what I thought was an aggressive goal of 70,000 steps in one week. On my fourth day in the program, I took 22,600 steps, approximately 10.8 miles. Granted, I mowed our large lawn, helped a neighbor move into a new home, and walked our dogs a few times that day; not exactly a normal day for me. At the end of the day, I'd logged approximately 10.8 miles. I couldn't believe it! I made my goal of 70,000 steps within my first week and set a more aggressive goal for the next week. I honestly never realized I had walked that far. My normal workdays yield more like three to four miles a day.

Today, I have a different perspective on my capabilities. I would not have guessed that I could have achieved these numbers if I hadn't tracked my progress daily. More importantly, this regular input on my progress gave me a reason to celebrate my success!

I already had some pretty good habits in place before I started measuring my footsteps. I don't sit when I talk on the phone in my office; I pace with a wireless headset on. I take regular breaks from my desk, and take a long walk after lunch. (I guess I have a problem sitting still.) But, I really liked being aware of the miles adding up and visualizing getting healthier every day.

After just a few weeks, I recognized that I had started to establish new habits and behaviors that changed my expectations (or perceptions) on what I was capable of achieving. In time, I became less conscious of this walking activity every day and made my walks a part of the "new me" and my personal plan. I still use the daily feedback to reinforce my positive behaviors, or let me know when I am off a bit. I can see myself achieving my goal and coming closer to attaining my wish.

Our Technique to Define and Set Checkpoints

Before you can define and set checkpoints toward your goals, you must understand how big of a stretch it is between where you are now and the achievement of each goal. In other words, you look at a goal you have set in support of one of your outcomes. You think about the gap between what you are currently doing relative to this goal and the measures you set for goal success. Is this gap pretty big? Is the completion time you set a month or more out? Now you can begin to create a mental picture of the milestones or incremental steps that you will need to take to achieve the goal.

In some cases, you may not really know the milestones and checkpoints that will make the most sense until you get started. In this case, you can estimate reasonable milestones and set up checkpoints and adjust them as you see what you can really do. In Dennis's personal example, he had guessed at 70,000 steps as a milestone and set a checkpoint at the end of his first week of aggressive walking. Considering that he had no idea what his current number of steps really was, 70,000 sounded pretty daunting. All he knew was that would be about 10,000 steps a day or a little less than five miles. He walks his dogs a few miles each day and doesn't sit still at his desk on most days so this seemed pretty reasonable, though a bit courageous. After he saw what he could really do, he adjusted his milestone and checkpoints accordingly.

By establishing reasonable, yet courageous checkpoints throughout the period of time in which you want to accomplish your goal, you can achieve success in a timely fashion. By "reasonable but courageous," we mean setting checkpoints that are feasible but push you a little. You will define courageous, of course; what is courageous for you may not be for someone else. And keep in mind that if you have more than one goal tied to an outcome, you will establish different checkpoints for each goal. This may sound a little tedious, but we promise it's not. You will probably find that your milestones run parallel to each other, because they are all intended to help you accomplish a single outcome. Figure 28 provides a graphic example.

WISH - to achieve 40 percent better physical and mental health scores from my Doctor by year's end

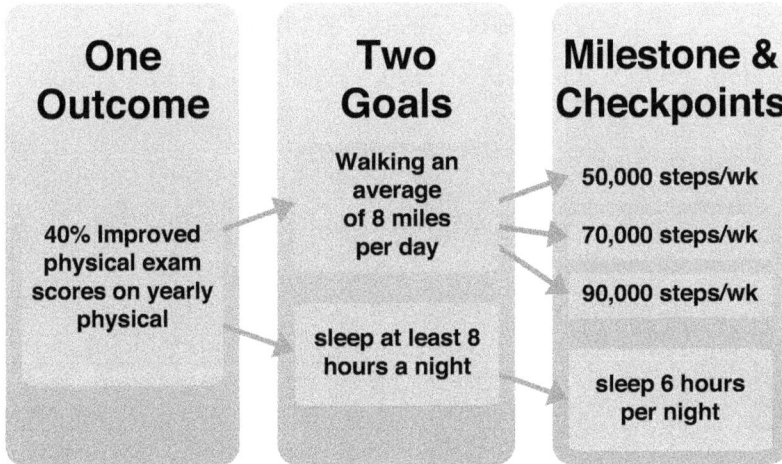

One Outcome	Two Goals	Milestone & Checkpoints
40% Improved physical exam scores on yearly physical	Walking an average of 8 miles per day	50,000 steps/wk
		70,000 steps/wk
		90,000 steps/wk
	sleep at least 8 hours a night	sleep 6 hours per night

Figure 28. Goals with Milestones & Checkpoints

Once you are able to visualize the milestones you will need for each goal, how often they occur, and the span of time over which they will occur, write these down. We have provided a *Goal Checkpoint and Milestone Worksheet* (illustrated in Figure 29) in the PDF worksheet packet to assist you.

Outcome:		
Goal:		
Milestone (Ex: 10,000 steps):	Checkpoint (by date, etc.):	Notes:
Milestone:	Checkpoint (date, etc.):	Notes:
Milestone:	Checkpoint (date, etc.):	Notes:
Goal:		
Milestone:	Checkpoint (date, etc.):	Notes:
Milestone:	Checkpoint (date, etc.):	Notes:
Milestone:	Checkpoint (date, etc.):	Notes:

Figure 29. Snapshot of the Goal Checkpoint and Milestone Worksheet

Remember, making this personal commitment to yourself is the first step in setting checkpoints. Now you are on your way. In the next sections we will show you how to use these checkpoints to monitor, gauge, and log your progress toward achieving a goal.

Using Checkpoints to Monitor, Gauge, and Log your Progress

After we have noted our checkpoints in our personal plan for breaking tape, what do we do with them? How do we monitor our progress and log how we are doing without making this a chore?

We advocate keeping your method for monitoring and gauging progress as simple as possible and tying related checkpoints together to minimize the number of things you are trying to monitor. Some people use technology (as Dennis used Fitbit), some keep paper handy, and some log a note on a phone or tablet. Choose a method that works for you and suits your lifestyle. Here are some tips and techniques to monitor, gauge, and log your progress:

- Keep a personal log on how well you are doing. This can be a strong motivator and an accurate gauge to see if you are actually making progress.

- Set a specific time every day to review your progress and reflect on how far you have come and what you will be doing next. Some people like doing this at the beginning of each day; others prefer the end of the day.

- Create a chart or graph of your milestones and checkpoints so that you can always see the big picture of your progress. Charts and graphs help you see that even if you had one bad day, overall, you are making the forward progress you need.

- Create and use a journal to track your progress. At least once a week, record notes about:
    o How you are doing at working toward your goals
    o Your plans to keep moving forward
    o Your feelings about successes and problems you are having
    o The new behaviors and positive habits you are forming as you make progress toward your goal

- If you made progress, take the time to think about what you did right before you focus on what you still need to do.

This will help you spot the conditions and actions that have helped you to move forward.

- Share your progress on a weekly basis with at least one other person who will help keep you accountable and motivate you to stay on track.

Whatever tips or tools you use, discipline yourself to keep on track until you achieve success. Capture the ideas and techniques you think will work for you on your *Goal Checkpoints and Milestones Worksheet*.

"There are many ways of going forward, but only one way of standing still." -
Franklin D. Roosevelt

Celebrate your Improvements and Checkpoint Achievements

Give yourself some credit! Now you have a really good reason to celebrate—achievement! We can't overemphasize the importance of this part of our WINNING Method—the idea of celebrating small, incremental milestones at checkpoints as you move ever closer to your goal. We all need a pat on the back once in a while, or to hear a simple "Congratulations" from a family member or peer at work.

We're not advocating that you throw a party at every checkpoint, which might be counterproductive in some cases. But we know the importance of acknowledging improvements and achievements. It is also important to share your accomplishments with the people who know you, who know what you are working toward.   Everyone is wired a bit differently in this regard.   The extrovert may post a picture on Facebook showing the world the jeans he used to wear before losing 10 pounds. The introvert may just share this progress with a partner or friend.   Either approach will work as a personal motivator and a simple celebration of your progress toward your goals.

Don't ignore the impact of celebration. Here's an example from Karen.

My family moved around a lot when I was small. So when I moved from one state to another, it was no surprise to discover that my new class was already doing multiplication tables. I had to do a lot of work to catch up with my new peers. I still remember the day I was able to celebrate success. My mom let me jump on the bed as I recited the entire multiplication tables. This was memorable (and motivating to my younger self) because it was not something I was normally allowed to do, and it was fun!

Find something that motivates you, is fun, or helps you signify an achievement in a special way. It could be a simple celebratory dance, going to a movie, or out to dinner. *Every* step toward achieving your goal, your outcomes, and eventually your wish, is important. Each achievement represents something you may not have done in the past. This is reason enough for a simple acknowledgement and celebration. These moments are little drivers, fueling the fire of your success. Like the second wind that long-distance runners describe, they give you that extra push toward breaking tape.

Closing Thoughts

As your goals come to fruition and you see that you are achieving your outcomes, the achievement of your wish is not far away! You are breaking tape!

Although in this chapter we have focused primarily on achievements and progress, please be aware that you may have some bumps in the road to success—we all do. Not all of our goals or milestones are easy to achieve and sometimes we fail before we succeed. Failing to achieve a goal or milestone on your way to success can be a teacher for you. In fact, we believe that every failure can be a step toward success if you learn from it. You might ask yourself:

- What did I do right?
- What went wrong?
- What would I do differently next time?
- I wonder if my role model could coach me on this one.
- What did I learn from this bump in the road?

Don't be afraid to re-set a goal's timeframe if you discover that it is either more complicated or challenging than you originally thought. It is more important that you find ways to continue to move forward than to meet every goal exactly within the timeframe you originally set. Finally, whatever troubles you face, don't forget to focus on the things that worked and went well and celebrate that success.

Your success is part of the reward. The other part is the journey to get you there and the opportunity to learn new habits and behaviors that create positive changes in your life. Throughout this seven-step WINNING Method, we have encouraged you to learn from your role model and set your sights high. In Part Three of this book, you will learn how to continue your growth and become a role model yourself, another important part of creating new habits and building on your personal plan for breaking tape.

If you haven't yet completed the *Goal Milestone and Checkpoint Worksheet*, please do so now and revisit your motivating factors by answering the questions in the motivational checkpoint.

Motivational Checkpoint

1. Are you comfortable moving forward with your plan to accomplish the milestones leading to your goals and outcomes?

2. Which goals are going to need more monitoring?

3. Do you have a plan in place in case you hit a bump in the road and a checkpoint or goal is not achievable at this time? What is your plan?

Work it Out

Apply the concepts and steps described in this chapter to complete this section of your personal plan for breaking tape.

Goal Checkpoint and Milestone Worksheet
Directions: Use the worksheet to document the goals, milestones, and checkpoints for each outcome that your wish requires. Use the prioritization you established in Step 6 as you enter your goals. Duplicate the worksheet as needed to enable you to capture all goals for each outcome.

PART THREE

Extending Your Success

Where Do You Go From Here?

"Try not to become a man of success, but rather try to become a man of value." – Albert Einstein, theoretical physicist

The Einstein quote may seem a bit odd for us to share with you now, near the end of the book. After all, throughout this book we've encouraged you to attain the success you wish for—at home or work. Yet, Einstein is correct with his fundamental truth. If you just aim for the shiny object, you might attain it, only to find yourself unhappy still. The truly successful people in work and life always give the same advice—true success means focusing not just on what you want, but also on the values that matter. It is for this reason that we advised you at the beginning of the WINNING Method to select a role model whose values align with yours. Now that you have achieved the wish you defined, let's make sure you keep this focus.

Bottom-line, success in itself is not the main goal in our lives. Yes, it's important to strive for a wish with a solid definition of success and to achieve goals that will help you attain your wish. But without passion, belief, and values, success can feel empty. We have talked throughout our book about the important virtues of passion, belief, and defining success through the lens of your values. Now, we want to reiterate these important ideas as you move forward. Live your 'values.' Make sure that both your current success and your next steps align with your values. Don't put the cart before the horse. The things that you value should continue to drive and enable your ability to be *truly* successful.

The purpose of this chapter is to encourage you to keep moving forward after your initial success. You have made your wish a reality! Many people will be thrilled just to have been successful. Others may experience elation after achieving something important, quickly followed by a sense of "Now what?" Some people may even experience a sense of letdown when they attain something they've worked hard for. This is why some say the journey is as important as reaching the goal. The first step is for you to acknowledge what you are feeling. The next step is to recognize that there is more to your life than attaining your wish.

Now, it's time to define what's next for you. So, you say you're perfectly satisfied enjoying your new success. Great, savor it with our congratulations! But if you desire to add more value to your own life or the lives of others, there is always more you can do. There are three powerful things to consider; you may even find this information to be one the most important parts of the book.

In this chapter you will learn:

- How to stay on track to maintain your achievements
- Tips for keeping great habits for life
- The importance of giving thanks and acknowledging the contributions of those who helped you.

Staying on Track

You've achieved your wish—*now* what? The good news is that your brain is now wired with some new behaviors. You've learned these behaviors as you met your new goals, produced outcomes, achieved your wish, and changed your life for the better.

Don't get too excited yet, however. The bad news is that your new behavior wiring is still fragile. The old behaviors you thought you left behind on your way to success are also wired in your brain, and they are more stable from years of use. These old behaviors don't exactly go away; they stay wired in your brain, alongside the new behaviors you have learned. In some ways, these two types of wiring are like roads running parallel to one another—you could take either road.

To keep these positive new behaviors in use, and your success on track, you must stay vigilant. That means revisiting, reviewing, and refining the outcomes and goals you set to attain your wish. After all, we humans don't stay the same; we continue to evolve personally, and to develop ourselves professionally. By keeping your outcomes and goals fine-tuned, you can maintain their relevance to your life. As you do so, you improve the likelihood that you will stay on track. At the same time, you keep your new, positive behaviors in the forefront of your brain. In time, and with continued success, your old behaviors will become a distant memory, like an unused road that nature obliterates.

How Do I Revisit, Review, and Refine My Outcomes and Goals?

You start with a simple plan and a continuing belief that what you are doing is valuable to you. Sounds simple – and it is, in a way. Repeating a new behavior over time, and getting positive reinforcement along the way, will help you through this process.

For some people, making a note on their weekly or daily to-do list to review their outcomes and goals is enough to cement their new behaviors and keep their outcomes and goals in check. For others, staying on track might require a more detailed look at where they are now, where they want to be in six months or a year, and refining their outcomes and goals to get them there.

Take the time to revisit and refine your personal plan for breaking tape. Review the outcomes and goals you set up when you began this process. If you want to keep them in check or advance them to a higher level, ask yourself the following questions:

- How am I going to keep my success drivers in place and roadblocks out of the way – forever?
- Based on what I want to do next, how should I redefine my wish, outcome, or goals? Maybe it's time to consider a new, more aggressive wish or set of outcomes.

- Do I need a different role model to help me refine my new wish and outcomes?
- Is the gap between where I am today and where I want to be possible or feasible to bridge?
- What new goals do I need to set to close the gap between where I am today and where I want to be?

Take the answers to these questions and begin refining and adjusting your personal plan for breaking tape, using the worksheets in the PDF worksheet packet.

Breaking tape using our WINNING Method is not an event that just happens once in your life. The WINNING Method has now become a part of your life, a way of life for achieving your wishes. When new habits and learned behaviors become the way you approach your life, you have a much greater probability of staying on track and achieving future successes.

How Do I Keep a Winner's Mindset?

When you make the WINNING Method a part of the way you approach your life, the things you desire will be easier to achieve over time. It is important to keep a winner's mindset as you move forward, either maintaining your achievement or setting new wishes and goals. Everyone will slip now and then, and some may temporarily lose their focus. Here are some tips to keep a winner's mindset and make your future success more likely. Figure 30 illustrates these suggestions.

- Incorporate the seven steps from the WINNING Method into everything you do in life. This is not as tough as it may seem. Once you've learned these steps, it is actually hard to turn them off. (Just ask our families.)

- Develop a can-do attitude. You have already achieved success. You have started learning new habits to use for future success. Acknowledge your success—you did it, and you can do it again. Reinforce these changes in your life. As you do so, you should begin to see challenges as opportunities. Now you know you can do it—you have achieved a wish before. With this, you are on your way to creating a winner's mindset.

- Begin thinking in terms of the outcomes you need to produce and not just behaviors. For example, as we type these words, we are writing a book—a behavior. But, we can't be satisfied with that. We have to stay focused on our primary outcome of *"A published book that is read by you and makes a difference in your life!"* Anybody can put words together and say they are writing a book. It is much more powerful to stay focused on the outcome of "a published book that makes a difference in people's lives." This is our focus. It is motivating. And it keeps us working toward the end result—an outcome of true value.

Dennis mentioned earlier that a 'healthier me' was an important outcome in his life, and eating right and walking a lot every day were behaviors on his way to that outcome. If he focused on individual behaviors such as eating right, he would not necessarily develop a winner's mindset because those behaviors were only a small piece of the puzzle.

Winners focus on the end result. They focus on the outcomes that lead to their wish. They practice and build on the behaviors that support these outcomes. This is an important difference. Many people know what they need to 'do,' yet few people focus on what they need to 'produce'—outcomes that lead to their wish. Once you get this mindset shift in your head (Figure 30), you will see success differently.

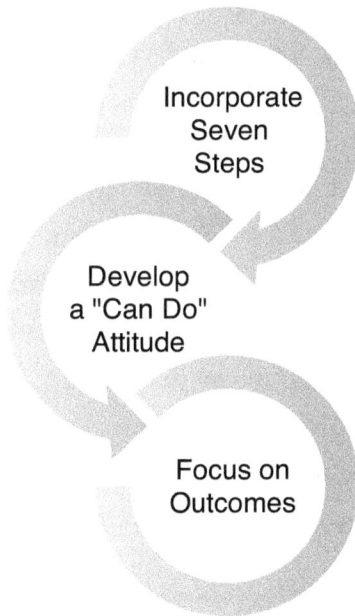

Figure 30. Developing a Winner's Mindset

Learn from This Experience How to Stay Motivated

Learn from your experiences how to keep yourself motivated and to continue to build new habits and positive behaviors for life.

Let's revisit an example we used earlier in this book. Can you remember when you could not ride a two-wheel bicycle? You learned how to ride that bike by watching your friends ride their bikes, and from the coaching your parents gave you as they ran next to you. And of course you learned from trial and error. All of these experiences shaped you and provided you with the skills and knowledge to be able to ride that two-wheel bike by yourself. You used the belief that you could do it and the drive to get it accomplished. And no doubt, you were VERY motivated to ride that bike and not much was going to stop you.

The same holds true for you as an adult. You have to tap into the same thinking and experiences for everything you learn and accomplish throughout your life. You will continue to learn from watching and asking others, getting coaching from role models, and from trial and error. With every success you achieve, you learn a little more about yourself, what works for you, and what motivates you. But remember, failure also can be a teacher if you examine why you failed and determine what you need to do differently to succeed next time.

"Success is not final, failure is not fatal; it is the courage to continue that counts."
- Winston Churchill, British prime minister and politician

All of our life experiences, both positive and negative, are a part of the path we travel to achieve what we desire, and to fulfill and develop ourselves as healthy adults. If we view them correctly, our learning experiences can also serve as motivators to get us another step closer to achieving our wishes.

What Would I Do if I Believed I Could Not Fail?

Ask yourself: "What would I do if I believed I could not fail?" What else have you wanted to do but haven't tried because you feared failure or didn't think you had the resources you needed? Turn a hobby into a business? Develop a new career? Get that college degree? Start a charity? Quit smoking? Write a book? Travel to another country? Run for office?

This is a powerful question that unlocks what is possible for you. It also can help you create larger outcomes and goals and take your wish to a new level. The only thing holding you back is yourself. So ask yourself right now: "What would I do if I believed I could not fail?"

Write your answers on the *Where Do I Go from Here Worksheet* in the PDF worksheet packet and take time to explore what is possible for you. This new list might include your next wish or a set of outcomes you want to achieve to build on your current wish. Go for it! Figure 31 is a snapshot of this worksheet.

Where Do I Go from Here Worksheet	
Staying on Track	
How am I going to keep my *success drivers* in place and *roadblocks* out of the way – forever?	Notes:
Based on what I want to do next, how should I redefine my wish, outcome, or goals? Consider a bigger wish or set of outcomes.	Notes:
Do I need a different role model to help me refine my new wish and outcomes?	Notes:
Is the gap between where I am today and where I want to be possible or feasible?	Notes:
What *new* goals do I need to set to close the gap between where I am today and where I want to be?	Notes:
Keeping a Winner's Mindset	
What am I doing to incorporate the seven steps from the WINNING Method into everything I do in life?	Notes:
What am I going to do to develop a can-do attitude to support my goals and outcomes?	Notes:
How will I practice thinking in terms of the outcomes I need to produce, and not just the behaviors I need to practice every day?	Notes:
Learning from this Experience and Keeping Myself Motivated	
What would I do if I believed I could not fail?	Notes:
What else have I wanted to do but haven't tried because I feared failure or didn't think I had the resources I needed?	Notes:
Identify my fear here, give it a name, and then embrace it.	Notes:
What is it going to take to overcome my fear?	Notes:
Giving Thanks to My Role Model	
What am I going to say to thank my role model?	Notes:
Who are the friends I would like to thank and what am I going to say to them?	Notes:

Figure 31. Snapshot of the Where Do I Go from Here Worksheet

Keeping Great Habits for Life

Most people who have accomplished great success wonder how they can make their new behaviors great habits for life. It is possible to create and keep great habits but it takes commitment and the desire to really make it happen.

New habits and behaviors become easier over time. Psychologists say that it takes 21 days to learn or adapt a new behavior. This is just a guideline; the number of days could be less or more for you. All we know for sure is that if you *practice* a behavior regularly, it more easily becomes a part of your life. If you desire a new behavior and commit mentally to the change, you have a much greater likelihood of success.

Whether you are trying to lose weight, exercise more, manage your work more effectively, or get that next promotion, you must first acknowledge that your old behaviors and habits may interfere with your success. Throughout this book, you have learned methods for acquiring new habits and behaviors that lead you to greater success. Now you need to practice them consistently. Try them out and get used to them. At first you will notice the difference between new and old behaviors. As you practice them and you see the rewards that new behaviors bring, you will also see that they keep you aligned with your goals and your wish. As this happens, new behaviors are reinforced and become rote, meaning we don't have to think about practicing them. Eventually, the new behavior becomes a part of your normal response pattern. Figure 32 illustrates this process.

New Behavior
Different from
established
behavior.

Feels odd at
first.

Practiced Behavior
Trying it out.
Getting used to it.
Using it consistently.

Reinforced Behavior
Seeing rewards
for the
behavior.

Behavior
becomes rote.

New normal
response
pattern.

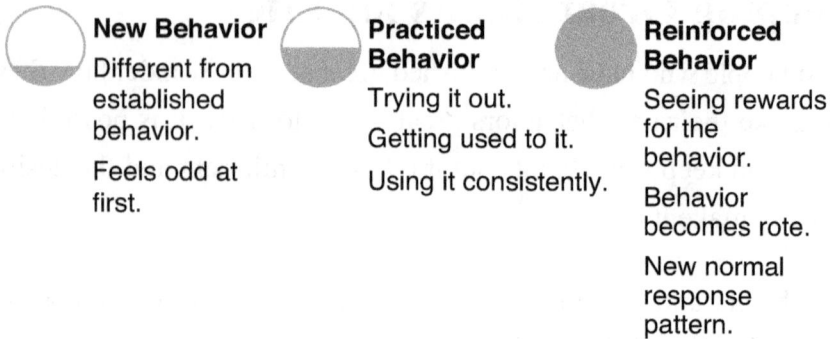

Figure 32. Making a new behavior stick

What if I Fall Back into My Old Habits?

It's true that you can still fall back into old habits even when you have a new behavior that has become routine and comfortable. This is because your old behaviors have not been eliminated completely from your memory and brain.

So accept that this can happen. It does not make you bad or weak, but if you let it, this can put a wedge between you and what you want in life. How should you respond? Choose to do what is best for you. Think about the hard work that went into meeting the goals and producing the outcomes that led to your success. Use the new behaviors, mindset, and attitude that you created on your way to success. And don't forget how important this success was for you. It still is!

If you fear falling back into old behaviors, talk to others, including your role model, and review your personal plan for breaking tape again. This is your roadmap to success. You may need to tweak your plan from time to time. It is an excellent reminder of what you need to focus on. Expect that it is possible to slip into old habits from time to time. But once good habits and behaviors are well established, this will happen less and less.

Surround yourself with people who are focusing on the same things you are in your success plan (or close to it). Finding people who understand your goals helps you stay on track. Get into a group of people who have similar attitudes, wishes, and goals because it is easier to reinforce your good new habits this way. Stay away from people who might reinforce poor habits and behaviors.

For example, we talked to a couple of very successful sales people selling a commodity in a down economy. They were doing very well when others on the sales team had dismal results. They chose not to hang out in the 'neighborhood' with the sales people with the poor results. Instead, they got together with each other over a cup of morning coffee to share their successes from the previous day. In other words, they created a new neighborhood that supported their success.

If in spite of such positive actions, you sense that your wish is slipping away, ask yourself: "What am I really afraid of?" For example, is it the fear of failure, the fear of success, or the fear of the changes and expectations that success could bring? If you start to feel fear moving in, take the following steps:
- Identify and name the fear, then face it head on
- Determine what it is going to take to overcome the fear and make a plan to do so
- Execute the plan, getting assistance if you need it.

Franklin D. Roosevelt understood fear and its affect on us. In his inaugural address at the height of the Great Depression in the 1930's, he said: "Let me assert my firm belief that the only thing we have to fear is fear itself—*nameless, unreasoning, unjustified* terror which paralyzes needed efforts..." Is your fear nameless? Does it make sense? Is it justified? It's time for you to stop letting fear control you. Embrace the fear, realize it can happen, but don't let it paralyze you. Your goals and success are much more important than what you fear.

Finally, your experience and the journey you took to accomplish your wish has opened up many possibilities for you in the future. Ask yourself: "What can I do *right now in support of my wish or my next wish* that would be the most powerful use of this moment? Write it down now in the *Where Do I Go from Here Worksheet.* Add it to your weekly to-do list. And tell others about what you are going to do.

Giving Thanks

There is someone very important to you who was central to how you created your personal plan for breaking tape—your role model! It's time to acknowledge and thank your role model for his or her input and support. Gratitude is an important part of having a positive attitude. Being grateful helps us focus on the positive things we have achieved and the people who helped us attain success.

Your role model was (and may continue to be) a key to your personal or work success. He or she provided you with guidance, insight, a model of success, coaching, and emotional support during your success journey. The least you can do is say "Thank you." How you say thank you is up to you. We know you understand that your thank you should be personal and realistic. It should come from your heart and express what your role model's contribution has really meant to you and your success.

By thanking your role model, you reinforce their decision to be a role model to you, which makes it more likely that they will repeat this behavior for others in the future. It also reinforces the behaviors, goals, and outcomes that led them to their own success, helping them stay on track for the long term. What a great way to offer something back to the person who helped you!

It is also time to share your success with others who helped you or gave you support along the way, such as family members, co-workers, and friends. Tell them how you did it, and how they contributed to your success. Thank them in your own words.

Maybe you have heard that by doing good for others, the good comes back to you in multiples. Giving thanks is part of the process of doing good. Also, share the methods, tools, and success tips that worked for you to help others achieve their success, too. Friends and family members like to hear about things that had a positive influence on your life, especially when they could apply them to their own lives too.

Closing Thoughts

We encourage you to continue to wish for things that you value in your life and that are important to you personally and professionally. We hope that you make the WINNING Method and its seven steps a part of your habits and behaviors for life! It will make a difference.

Life will toss you some curve balls from time to time, and there will be some failures along the way to your success. You can't avoid them; challenges are part of life. To your advantage, you now have a method that you can use to address such challenges and stay on track for future successes.

Motivational Checkpoint

1. What have I learned about myself from the experience of breaking tape?

2. Whom do I need to thank for their assistance?

3. In what areas do I need to be vigilant so that I don't fall back on old habits and behaviors?

Work it Out

Apply the concepts and steps described in this chapter to complete this section of your personal plan for breaking tape.

Where Do I Go from Here Worksheet

Directions: Use this worksheet in the PDF worksheet packet to document your plan and ideas for your next steps.

Becoming a Role Model for Others

"By being a living role model of what you want to receive from others, you create more of what you want in your life."
– Eric Allenbaugh, author and facilitator

You made your wish a reality and you have a plan for staying on track to maintain your success! Congratulations! You put everything together—your dreams, motivation, tips from your role model, support from others, and your hard work—to achieve success. You have earned the right to celebrate your success. ***We think you also have earned a responsibility to become a role model, sharing with others what you've learned.*** We know what you're thinking—you're glad you worked hard and made your wish a reality, but you wouldn't say that qualifies you to be a role model.

We highly encourage you to act as a role model to others, and in doing so, you will continue to grow personally and professionally. Remember, although you have come a long way and worked hard to achieve your goals and wish, you did not do it alone. By following the WINNING Method, you had a role model to get you started on the right track. Your role model may have provided continual support and tips to keep you on track. He or she may even have helped you get back on track after a misstep or failure. We hope so, because this is where the value of having a role model lies.

You probably have thanked your role model already, but you realize it is impossible to really pay them back. You can't put a monetary figure on their important contribution. Instead, you can "pay it forward" by serving as a role model for someone else. Whether you realize it or not, people you know have already taken note of your success. They saw how hard you worked. They are happy for you and they have seen what you have accomplished. Some of them may even be motivated by you and your success to work toward their own wishes. In you, they see possibilities for themselves.

> *"Others see their possibility in the reality of you. Your message is your life lived."*
> *– Neale Donald Walsch, author*

You may be thinking, "Me, a role model?" Yes, you *can* be a role model! In fact, whether you realize it or not, you may already be a role model to someone else. Not in a formal sense, perhaps, but we're betting that someone is already looking up to you for your guidance or expertise. We all do this. Worried that you're not perfect, or that you are not an expert? You don't have to be! You don't have to know all the answers. Who does? A role model is an example—someone who has achieved something we value, done something we value, or behaved in ways we value. Now *you* can add value to someone else's life by acting as their role model.

In this chapter you will learn:

- Why it's important to become a role model for others
- How to become a role model for others.

Why It's Important to Become a Role Model for Others

There is an old saying that there's no better teacher than experience. You've applied the WINNING Method to help you achieve the wish you desire. Now, we challenge you to extend your success by paying it forward and helping others.

You can extend your own success by helping others who want to achieve something similar to your wish or other things that you have accomplished in your life. Acting as a role model to others obviously benefits them and indirectly, your community or workplace. But, acting as a role model also has several very positive benefits for *you*, including:

- Reinforces the good changes you made for yourself
- Helps keep you from going back to bad habits
- Encourages behaviors which lead to success
- Helps you to be more aware of yourself, both at work and at home.

"Example has more followers than reason."
- Christian Nevell Bovee, author and
lawyer

Although you have attained your wish and established new, more positive behaviors, you may be tempted to fall back on behaviors that are *not* so positive. As we mentioned before, habits—especially old ones—can be hard to break. We have them hard-wired in our brains.

But if you are acting as a role model and serving as an example to others, you are more aware of yourself and your behaviors, and more motivated to persist with good habits. In a way, being a role model to someone else completes the cycle of your success, as illustrated by Figure 33. By making your wish a reality, your self-image and attitude improves. You have proven yourself to be an achiever and have worked hard to get the results you wanted.

When you make your wish a reality, you experience the work or life success you desired as you began this journey. As you reach out to others and act as a role model to them, you share your success with them and reinforce your own successes and positive attitude. By providing to others the kind of tips and guidance you received, you help them succeed. In turn, your attitude and self-image further improve.

Figure 33. Cycle of Success

Finally, being a role model for others feels good and it's good for you, too. Who doesn't want to feel good about themselves once in a while? The rewards of giving back and helping others really cannot be measured. The true measure of a person is not the wealth or things he or she leaves behind, but the lives he or she touched in a positive way.

"If there be any truer measure of a man than by what he does, it must be by what he gives."
- Robert South, English churchman

How Do I Become a Role Model to Others?

OK, we've convinced you (or perhaps we just wore you down)! So, what's the process for moving from "doer" to "role model?" The process is a natural one. In fact, the people who need you as a role model will find you. You just have to be ready, make yourself available to others, and be able to assist them. Think about the following as you determine how you can become a role model to others.

1. What opportunities do you have to be a role model? Who looks up to you? Who has already taken note of the success you achieved? Has this person already approached you or asked to meet with you?

2. Take some time for self-reflection. How do you think someone's life can be better because they cross your path? What are you willing to model and commit to doing?

3. What special methods, tips, or techniques did you learn from your experience that you could share with others?

4. What did the role model you selected do to make a difference to your success? Are you willing to do the same for others? How did the role model act to put you at ease or convey an important message?

5. There is always room for individuality—you need not become a mirror image of your role model to be a good one. What special perspectives or skills do *you* have beyond what your role model offered you?

Do I Have What It Takes?

Anyone can be a role model—the real question is whether or not you will be a *good* one! Many of the skills it takes to be an effective role model are similar to those required for coaching, managing, and being a good friend. Be the role model you would like to have as your friend or coach!

Figure 34 illustrates skills that characterize effective role models.

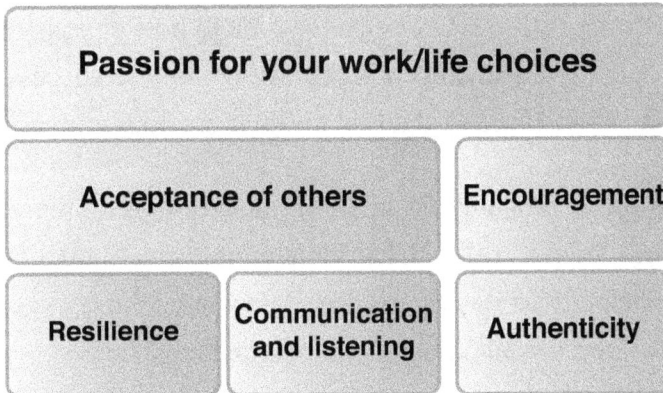

Figure 34. Skills for Effective Role Models

Passion for your work/life choices—Effective role models are excited by, and passionate about, their work/life choices, including their achievements and the difference they have made. They often commit to becoming more active in their neighborhood, church, synagogue, or community to share their passion and talents to benefit others.

Acceptance of others—A role model must be willing to accept others where they stand. You could also say this is meeting people where they are, mentally and physically. The goal is not to make the people you are helping "love you"—the goal is to offer guidance to help them succeed. Like you, they won't be perfect, but they want to make a change for the better. We don't need to change them to think or be like us: We just need to add value.

Encouragement—Think about the best coach you ever had in sports, school, or at work. We're willing to bet that while they challenged you, (maybe a lot) they did so in an encouraging way. You're not doing this to win a prize, or even to bolster your resume. You are doing it to help someone achieve *his or her* success. Your encouragement will be like the fuel for their success engine.

Resilience—You probably faced an obstacle or two on the journey to make your wish a reality. Chances are, your role model or other supporters helped you stay the course when you hit those roadblocks. An effective role model not only demonstrates resilience in the face of obstacles: They also inspire it in the people they assist.

Communication and listening—Good role models communicate effectively and that doesn't mean they do all the talking. In fact, the most effective role models will talk less than the people they are helping. They ask the right questions, probing to reveal truths and previously unspoken fears. They listen actively, not diagnostically. Role models don't need to fix things, but they need to demonstrate that they hear others and use body language that supports what they are saying. A good role model confirms options, and maybe even provides options that the people they are helping were not aware of.

However, the decision of what to do next belongs to the person with the wish, not to the role model.

Authenticity—Great role models know that they must be themselves. We're all human. You don't have to know all the answers. Remember, nobody's perfect—including role models.   Authenticity simply means that you are genuine, trustworthy, and true to yourself. It doesn't mean you have to share all of your dirty laundry, but it does mean that you must be honest in sharing what did and did not go right.   By doing so, the people you help benefit from your lessons learned.

Being authentic is the easiest thing to do and the most difficult thing to do.   The difference: people who are authentic show it in their voices, their eyes, and their body language. When you try hard to be authentic and you are not, your body language is not in synch with your words.   We're sure you have seen what we are talking about. For example, your supervisor says he wanted to find ways to streamline production. But when you suggest a time-saving idea, he nods at you while crossing his arms, frowning, and tapping his foot. A co-worker tells you "There is nothing to worry about; the project is on time," though he is not able to look you in the eye when he says it and his body language puts distance between you. In these two examples, the words just don't connect with the body language.

Setting the Right Example

As a role model, you are always setting an example for others whether you know it or not. Why not set the right example? This not only makes you a better role model, and improves the benefit you provide to others, but it also helps others see how they could be role models.

Here are some tips to maximize your effectiveness by setting the right example:

- As Mark Twain said, "Keep away from people who would belittle your ambitions." Surround yourself with supportive people who will continually help you become your best.
- Provide honest, descriptive feedback to help others stay on track, encouraging them to keep moving forward, even when they fail.
- Demonstrate your personal resilience. We said earlier that resilience was an important skill for role models. It's even more powerful when you demonstrate it to the people you are helping. Into every life a little rain will fall. Things will not always go well—for you or the people to whom you are a role model. Show them that temporary missteps and roadblocks need not derail a wish.
- Keep your commitments to those who see you as a role model. If you have set a meeting with them, be there. They are depending on you. Never promise to do something or meet with them on a specific date or time when you know that you cannot deliver.

- If you make a mistake, or feel you may have given advice you regret, own up to it. Don't cover up a mistake or blame them. This is powerful!
- Be aware of how you respond to change or events that shake the status quo. We all have a tendency to watch how our role models at work and home respond when something new or different (good or bad) happens.

Closing Thoughts

Living life fully requires that we reach out and help others. Giving back and sharing your success, and what you learned along the way, is a natural next step for you.

Think you have nothing to share? Don't be shy about what you have to offer. Just revisit your wish, outcomes, and goals to see how far you've come. Recall conversations you had with your role model and the points in your journey when these conversations made the most difference. If you have a friend or co-worker who is curious about the WINNING Method, loan them your copy of *Breaking Tape* so they can read it themselves. Then suggest that when they get to the chapter on selecting a role model, you will be ready.

Maybe you don't think you are ready to commit to being a role model for someone throughout his or her journey. Your success may still be too new to you and you may want to make sure it sticks first. You can at least share with others how you attained your wish. You've learned how to apply the WINNING Method to attain the success you desired. Share the method with them to help them get off to a good start. This is a great first step!

Motivational Checkpoint

1. In what areas do I feel I could be a role model for others?

2. Who can benefit from my experience?

3. What benefits could I gain through paying forward what I have learned?

A Note of Thanks from the Authors

We're taking our own advice and thanking our readers for investing time and energy in our book and in the WINNING Method. We know there are many books available for helping people achieve their goals and achieve success, and we appreciate that you chose ours.

We hope you were able to follow our WINNING Method all the way through to breaking tape on the personal or professional success you desired. We appreciate the faith you have in yourself and in the ideas we shared throughout the book.

We would love to keep in touch with you. We want to continue sharing tips for achieving success, and that includes hearing *your* ideas. We believe that the day we stop learning is the day we hang up our spurs, put the horse away, and stop teaching. We know that you can't teach others if you are afraid to learn yourself—and we are always willing to learn from others.

Also, we hope that you will consider being a part of one of our lectures, forums, and workshops on *Breaking Tape*. We'd be pleased to bring a workshop to your organization to share the WINNING Method with your colleagues. Here are a few ways you can keep in touch with us:

- By email for Dennis or Karen: Author@breakingtape.com
- Our website and blog: **http://breakingtape.com/**
- On Facebook: **www.facebook.com/BreakingTape**
- Follow Karen on Twitter at: @Performance_Doc